#1 *NEW YORK TIMES* BESTSELLING AUTHOR

MIKE EVANS

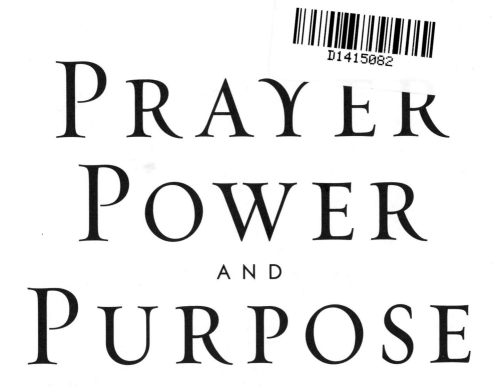

PRAYER
POWER
AND
PURPOSE

TimeWorthy BOOKS

P.O. Box 30000, Phoenix, AZ 85046

Prayer, Power and Purpose

Copyright © 2014 by Michael D. Evans

Time Worthy Books
P. O. Box 30000
Phoenix, AZ 85046

All rights reserved. No portion of this book may be reproduced, stored in a retrieval system, or transmitted in any form or by any means—electronic, mechanical, photocopy, recording, or any other—except for brief quotations in printed reviews, without the prior permission of the publisher.

Design: Peter Gloege | LOOK Design Studio

Hardcover: 978-1-62961-030-6
Paperback: 978-1-62961-031-3
   Canada: 978-1-62961-032-0

Unless otherwise indicated, scripture quotations are taken from the *King James Version* of the Bible.

Scripture quotations marked AMP are taken from *The Amplified Bible*, Old Testament copyright © 1965, 1987, by the Zondervan. The Amplified New Testament copyright © 1958, 1987 by The Lockman Foundation. Used by permission.

Scriptures marked NCV are taken from *The Holy Bible: New Century Version*, Containing the Old and New Testaments. Copyright © Word Bibles 1991. Used by permission.

Scriptures marked NASB are taken from the *New American Standard Bible*. Copyright © The Lockman Foundation 1960, 1962, 1963, 1968, 1971, 1972, 1973, 1975, 1977, 1995. Used by permission.

Scripture quotations marked NIV scripture quotations are taken from the H*oly Bible, New International Version*.® NIV®. Copyright © 1973, 1978, 1984, by International Bible Society. Used by permission of Zondervan Publishing House. All rights reserved.

Scripture quotations marked NLT are from *The Holy Bible, New Living Translation*, copyright ©1996. Used by permission of Tyndale House Publishers, Inc., Wheaton, Illinois, 60189. All rights reserved.

Scripture quotations marked TEV are from *The Holy Bible: Today's English Version*, 2nd ed. Copyright ©1992 by American Bible Society. Used by permission.

Scripture quotations marked THE MESSAGE are from *The Message*, copyright ©1993, 1994, 1995. Used by permission of NavPress Publishing Group.

Dedicated to

. . . those who are hungry and thirsty;
those who are willing to pay any price
until Jesus is so fully manifested in their lives
that the shadow they cast is not theirs
but the shadow of Jesus,
which causes a lost world to follow them
with a dying passion,
knowing that they have
"been with Jesus."

. . . to those whose heart's cry is
"Less of me,
all of Him."

Introduction

➤➤ ◂◂

In the Mid-1980s I was rushing through an airport in Rome with a friend of mine who was a television producer. Suddenly, I spotted at the opposite end of the tunnel a short, stooped woman wearing a familiar robe.

"Paul," I called to my friend, "Watch our stuff." I threw my bags at his feet and ran to her.

"My name is Mike Evans," I said as I approached, offering my hand to shake hers. Mother Teresa's dark eyes twinkled as she grasped my outstretched hand and said, "Mr. Evans, it is very nice to meet you."

All the love of the universe seemed to drain from the atmosphere at that moment. It was as if that love was concentrated within her tiny frame and radiated through her. My flight and my friend no longer existed. Like a schoolboy, I stammered a few words about my current mission to Israel, then collected myself and asked about her recent trip to the United States. I thought I would sympathize with her for returning to the suffering in India after enjoying the comforts of the States for a short time.

"No, no," she said with a sad smile. "It is in the United States that I am sad. I believe it is the poorest country on earth."

"But why?" I asked, stumbling in my attempt at small talk with this giant of faith.

"Ah," she said, "the United States is poor in spirit, and that is the worst kind of poverty."

I have meditated on Mother Theresa's profound statement in the years since that encounter, and have come to understand it more each day. In a land of wealth and opulence, with every opportunity afforded us—from timesaving gadgets to life-enhancing luxuries— our nation as a whole seems devoid of true fulfillment and lasting contentment. Even with all our computer-age technology, state-of-the-art communications satellites, multi-million dollar universities, and Internet-ready cell phones, we still don't seem able to rise to a level of greatness equal to our level of wealth. Like a good dream that doesn't last until morning, personal peace is fleeting and achieving a fulfilling purpose for living eludes us. We seem a nation of people who, while struggling to know our divine destiny, settle instead for complacency.

Yet within our hearts, destiny still calls. Somehow we know we were meant for something greater than what we are now living, but are not sure what it is or how to experience it.

Some of Jesus Christ's final words as He left this earth were, "All power in heaven and in earth is given unto me, so go and make followers of all people in the world. . . . I will be with you always," (Matthew 28:18-20 ncv.) He also promised that Christians would do greater works than He did because He went "unto the Father." (See John 14:12.) He promised that signs and wonders would follow his Believers. (See Mark 16:16-20.) One of the most puzzling things about becoming a Christian today is to read those promises, yet not experience them in our own lives. This is spiritual poverty.

New Christians are initially excited about their newfound faith, eager to seek God's favor and will for their lives. Now that they know there is a God and that He is the One who created the entire universe, they read their Bibles hoping to live every scripture in it. For a while, many do live in this power and can never imagine doing anything but what God has set before them. But then, other concerns and desires begin to creep in, and they are stymied. Somehow they meet disappointment in something they were hoping for, and they start making excuses. They look around the church and settle in to the norm they have experienced there, measuring spirituality by those they see around them. They begin to slowly forget or explain away the life of the supernatural they thought they had signed up for when they first pledged to follow Christ. They simply settle for less. Again, this is spiritual poverty.

Yet the promises and prayers of Jesus don't call us to live lives stained by such mediocrity and impotence. His prayers for His followers are that their lives will be marked by the intimacy of His relationship with His Father and alive with the works of His Spirit. If Jesus prayed this, wouldn't you think it should be coming to pass in our lives?

After all, no one in history is credited with answering more prayers than Jesus Christ. During His earthly ministry, the most amazing answers to prayer were recorded: From people born blind receiving their sight to the disabled suddenly leaping and walking— even the dead being raised back to life again. Since His crucifixion, millions have testified to having their prayers answered by calling on His name. His is still the largest crusade ever birthed on the planet with roughly two billion followers today. However written plainly in the ancient texts of the Bible are prayers that were prayed by Jesus Himself, yet have never been fully answered. Is there some connection between this and our spiritual poverty?

On the night before His crucifixion, Jesus gathered His disciples in an upper room in Jerusalem to be in their company one last evening and prepare them for what lay ahead. John in chapters 13-17 recorded the events that took place in that room, and this passage is among the greatest sections of teaching in the Bible. Jesus ended that evening with a prayer not only for those with Him at the time, "but for them also which shall believe on me through their [the disciples] word," (John 17:20.) In this prayer are nine specific requests that have never fully come to pass in the lives of Christ's disciples or in the generations that have followed. Why did the One who is considered the source of answered prayer leave with some of His own prayers unfulfilled? I can assure you that they will be answered, but when, how, and by whom?

I have asked myself these questions over and over in my more than four decades of ministry. During that time, God has taken me around the world to face great leaders. I have seen God do incredible things. I have experienced the spiritual poverty of which Mother Teresa spoke, but I have also experienced the spiritual abundance those in the book of Acts lived out through simple obedience. I have seen God heal the sick and disabled, miraculously open doors to meet government officials, and use me and others to work His will in ways I could never have imagined. If I have read my Bible correctly, these incredible things should not be considered unusual in the lives of those who follow Christ. These are the works every Believer is called to do according to the scriptures. Yet only a few Believers I have known have left such signs and wonders in their wake. It is my belief that the answers to the points of the prayers of Jesus in John 17 will only be realized when more rise up to walk in this spiritual abundance and are unwilling to settle for the spiritual lack that seems to grip most of Western Christianity. Are we willing to set aside our complacency to be part of the answer to His prayers?

Though Christian denominations differ on many points of faith, there seems to be one thing we share in common. We all believe that God answers prayer; yet, how can any of us have confidence in the prayers we offer to Him? This is either the greatest challenge to the faith for Christians today, or it is the greatest mystery in the Bible— and solving it is the paramount key to living the supernatural life we hope to have—the key to breaking out of spiritual poverty and into the fullness of Christ. (See Ephesians 4:13-16.)

I don't know about you, but that's the type of life I want to live—a life that will be part of the solution to that mystery and an answer to the prayers of Jesus. That's the Christian life I signed up for, and by God's grace, it is the life I have experienced too often to be willing to settle for anything less.

—Dr. Mike Evans

➤➤   ◄◄

CHAPTER ONE

What We Signed Up For

All power is given unto me in heaven and in earth.
Go ye therefore, and teach all nations. . . . I am with
you alway, even unto the end of the world.

MATTHEW 28:18-20

Go into all the world, and preach the gospel to every creature. . .
And these signs shall follow them that believe; In my name
shall they cast out devils; they shall speak with new tongues;
. . . they shall lay hands on the sick, and they shall recover.

MARK 16:15, 17-18

THE DAY AND TIME I FIRST received an inkling of what Jesus wanted to do in my life is unforgettable. It was 2:25 p.m. on October 19, 1967. I was sitting in the office of Professor Harris at the Bible College I attended looking at the clock on the wall behind his head.

I was a frustrated young man, and could not understand what God wanted for my life. Because of my Jewish background, I'd risked my relationship with my family in order to become a Christian, and now there seemed to be nothing I could do as a Believer. I was suffering from spiritual poverty and was unaware of it.

"I don't like church," I confessed to him. It seemed to be the only answer to what was wrong in my life. I sat through lessons, went to Bible studies, and attended services every time one was held, but I was still deeply dissatisfied. *Was this all there was to being a Christian?*

I talked a bit more with my professor as I fumbled in my efforts to better explain these feelings. At the end of voicing my dissatisfaction with much of what I had experienced as a Christian, he admonished me, "You'd better think twice about going into the ministry!" And then he added, "Let's pray."

As we bowed to pray, immediately the Lord reminded me, "If two or more shall agree as touching any one thing, I will do it." (See Matthew 18:19.) Realizing this was an opportunity for such an agreement in prayer, I decided to hold nothing back. I surrendered all of my life to Christ in a way I'd never done before.

When my beloved professor and I finished praying, he said, "Mike, just find a church and be faithful."

I nodded my head and left, determining in my heart to do much more with Christ's promises than just being faithful to a local church.

Perhaps in expressing my dissatisfaction with all I had experienced of the Christian life in his office that day, I realized that if all I ever did was hear *about* Christ's power and never *experience* it, I would be forever disillusioned—a condition in which many Christians find themselves today. I knew after all I had risked to enlist as one of Christ's soldiers I could never simply fill a vacancy in the pew of my local church and feel that I'd accomplished anything at all. I became aware that He died for much more than my privilege to sit in church, sing a few songs, and listen to some "feel good" sermons. I wanted to do what I'd signed up for—to experience the life Jesus had lived!

TIME FOR A REALITY CHECK

Anyone who reads the Gospels realizes that, for the great majority of Christians today, we are experiencing very little of what happened regularly during the life and ministry of Jesus. Then, if you go on to read the book of Acts, you have to question what the Church did to become unplugged from the power that had been experienced. Miracles and visions were a regular part of first-century Christianity. Why doesn't the Church live like that today?

Many have said that it is simply because God ordained miracles for that era, and now we are living in a different time, or dispensation of God's activity, when we need to have faith without seeing miracles. That makes sense if you look at circumstances today. In fact it makes many wish they had lived in the times of Jesus so that they might receive the help they need. If we could just see Jesus—if we could just touch Him—then everything would be better. If we could just walk with Jesus as the disciples walked with Him, then maybe we would also have the power of God available the way it was to the twelve apostles. Many believe the reason we don't experience the help needed is that things are different than when Jesus walked the earth with His disciples.

Yet, if you read what Jesus said to His disciples on the night before He was crucified, you realize that things today are different, but not in the ways we may have traditionally thought. Jesus never said anything about the miracles He performed being just for that time or there being different eras of God's grace. In fact, Jesus told His disciples that God had much more power for them to walk in *after* He left than what they were experiencing as they walked with Him during His earthly ministry.

How can I say this? Because Jesus himself told them, "It is better for you that I go away," (John 16:7 NCV.) He also said, "He that believeth on me, the works that I do shall he do also; and greater works than these shall he do; *because I go unto my Father,*" (John 14:12, italics added.) There were no time limits set on this. It was something that those who believed on Him would experience, and it wouldn't happen until *after* He ascended.

Look again at what Jesus said to His disciples at the end of the book of Matthew:

> *All power is given unto me in heaven and in earth. Go ye therefore, and teach all nations, baptizing them in the name of the Father, and of the Son, and of the Holy Ghost: Teaching them to observe all things whatsoever I have commanded you: and, lo, I am with you alway, even unto the end of the world,* (Matthew 28:18-20.)

Many of you are familiar with this passage called "the Great Commission," Jesus' instructions to His disciples—and to us—that we take the Gospel to the ends of the earth before He comes again. How many of us have heard this passage quoted in sermons about evangelism or missions and been told that this is God's commandment to tell others about Jesus? When we deny the power of which He tells us, we deny the very basis and implication of the scripture: "All the power of heaven and earth has been given to me, *therefore you go* and make disciples . . . because I—and all of that power given to me—will always be with you, even until the end of the world." Doesn't this imply that it is *because* we have the power of God with us that we should go and make disciples, and not that we should go and make disciples without it?

Mark records this in a similar way:

Go ye into all the world, and preach the gospel to every creature. He that believeth and is baptized shall be saved; but he that believeth not shall be damned. And these signs shall follow them that believe; In my name shall they cast out devils; they shall speak with new tongues; They shall take up serpents; and if they drink any deadly thing, it shall not hurt them; they shall lay hands on the sick, and they shall recover, (Mark 16:15-18.)

In other words, miraculous signs—devils cast out, people speaking in languages foreign to them, poisonous serpents being shaken off without causing harm (see Acts 28:3-6), and attempts made on the lives of His followers having no effect on them—would follow those that believed on Jesus' name.

Why is this? Jesus made it plain on that night before his crucifixion:

I will pray the Father, and he shall give you another Comforter, that he may abide with you for ever. . . .

These things have I spoken unto you, being yet present with you. But the Comforter, which is the Holy Ghost, whom the Father will send in my name, he shall teach you all things, and bring all things to your remembrance, whatsoever I have said unto you, (John 14:16, 25-26.)

I tell you the truth; It is expedient for you that I go away: for if I go not away, the Comforter will not come unto you; but if I depart, I will send him unto you, (John 16:7.)

While Jesus was on the earth, He had the Spirit of God—the Holy Spirit—without measure (see John 3:34)—all the power of God and His wisdom wrapped up in one Man in one place—but once He ascended, the Holy Spirit would then live in the hearts of all Believers around the world. The implication is not only that the disciples would be better off when Jesus left, but also that those who believe on Jesus because of their preaching would be better off than when Jesus walked the earth. If we had walked with Jesus as His disciples did, we would have had access to the power of God whenever we were with Him, just as the woman with the issue of blood received her wholeness when she touched the hem of His garment (see Mark 5:25-34). But now that He has ascended to the right hand of the Father, we have that same power of God within each of us in the Person of the Holy Spirit. This is how we are to walk in the greater works—through the Holy Spirit who lives inside every Believer.

Has the Holy Spirit gone away? Had this been the case, then it would be logical to also say that so have the works He did through Jesus and the disciples. If the Holy Spirit is still here in our time as He was in theirs, then the gifts of the Holy Spirit in which they walked must be available to us as well.

But if this is true, why aren't we experiencing these gifts as they did? When was the last time any of us experienced this miracle-working power? It would seem logical to assume that something has changed because we don't see the miracles Jesus and the disciples manifested anymore.

I might well have agreed with those that say miracles are not for today, had my simple hunger for more of God—my dissatisfaction with the *status quo*—not led me, rather by accident, to experiences indicating that Jesus' words haven't changed through the centuries. Somehow, in spite of myself, I have seen Jesus operate the same today as He did when He walked the earth. This has led me to see that for those who will make themselves available, the Holy Spirit will work just the same today as He has in every century since Jesus ascended to the Father.

GOD WANTS TO WORK THROUGH YOU AS HE DID THROUGH JESUS

In the late 1970s, I was asked to hold a one-night crusade in Lake Charles, Louisiana. This was after several weeks of travel, which had left me absolutely exhausted. A little girl with blue eyes and blonde pigtails, sat on the front row holding a bag on her lap. Her leg bones were so curved that her feet were twisted upward, forcing her to walk on her ankles.

Before she came that night, she had learned I was Jewish, which in her mind made me just like Jesus. Before the service, she insisted that her mother buy her a new pair of pink shoes to bring to the meeting. She believed she would need shoes to wear after her feet were healed. In the bag on her lap were those new shoes.

I had never witnessed a healing from such a severe deformity in any of my services. Did I have enough power or faith for her to be healed? What if she was disappointed when she evidently had such faith? At the close of the meeting, I prayed for everyone in the building leaving her for last, hoping many in the congregation would have left. When I looked, they were still there.

Finally, I picked her up and placed her on a little table next to me. I was so afraid of what was not going to happen that I closed my eyes as tightly as I could and at first silently prayed, "God I'm so exhausted and I don't feel as if I have an ounce of faith." My flesh, which had already assumed full responsibility, was telling me, "You're too tired to sense the Holy Spirit. Nothing is going to happen. You're going to be embarrassed. She'll go away disappointed."

Still, I prayed, asking God for her healing. The silence was shattered by the screams and cries of those in attendance. I thought, "This congregation surely has compassion for this little girl." I didn't open my eyes because I was afraid to look. Suddenly, the pastor shook my arm saying, "Open your eyes, open your eyes, and see what God has done!"

When I did open my eyes, there in front of me was the little girl wearing her new pair of pink shoes. Her ankles and legs were straight and normal!

Why had I thought it had anything to do with me? The little girl had the faith and God was the miracle worker—not me. What a lesson I learned that evening as I fell to my knees and asked God to forgive me for thinking I had any power to heal.

Jamie Buckingham, a journalist and friend, invited me to join him on an eleven-day trip to the Sinai Desert to retrace the footsteps of Moses. On the sixth day, we came upon a Bedouin family. The Arab woman had heard that a doctor, Angus Sargeant, was in our group. As we approached the encampment, the woman ran to us in tears, clutching her child in her arms.

The little six-year-old girl had fallen into a fire, and approximately one-third of her head was covered with a huge abscess. As a result, she was burning up with fever, and in great pain. As the woman begged the doctor for medicine, he turned to us and said, "This is a hopeless situation. I have no medicine that I can give the girl. She needs surgery, or she may die."

We learned that others in the Bedouin camp had taken hot knives to the child's face in an attempt to kill the infection. Instead, the little girl's face had been terribly scarred.

As I thought of my own three precious daughters, the compassion of Christ came upon me. I reached out my hand, and placed it on that green abscess, covered with flies. I began to intercede earnestly for this mother's daughter. In the natural, nothing happened.

We left the camp, and headed toward Mount Sinai. Angus turned to the group, and said, "I must go back. I have to operate on that child, and try to save her." A professional photographer in our group, Skip Jones, had taken a picture of the little girl. He decided to return with Angus and me. Angus entered the tent, and within a few moments, we could hear him crying. Skip and I peeked in the tent, and saw Angus with a rusty cup filled with polluted water.

As the Arab mother wept, he had lifted the cup to Jesus, and was praying, "Lord, I don't want to offend this woman by not drinking from the cup she has offered me. It is all she has." The offering she had given to Angus was her best offering. It was her expression of gratitude, for by her side was the same little girl – except there was no abscess, there were no scars. The child had been completely and miraculously healed. Angus did not have to operate. Skip took a second picture of the child, and we leapt for joy, and blessed the Lord for His mercy and compassion.

Through such experiences, I began to realize that Jesus had other intentions for the way His Church should operate in this day and age. His plan was not that we would be so defeated and despondent that the world would look down on us—that we would be so full of spiritual poverty that you couldn't tell us from those in the world who live without hope.

➤➤ ◄◄

CHAPTER TWO

The Prayer of Jesus for *All* His Followers

*These words spake Jesus, and lifted up his eyes to
heaven, and said, Father, the hour is come...*

JOHN 17:1

THE BEST PASSAGE that describes how Jesus wanted His
disciples to live in the Age following His ascension, what many call
the Church Age—the time between His ascension and His second
coming—is the prayer He prayed for His disciples in John 17. Take
a moment to read this passage and see if any of it sounds like what
you are experiencing in your life and your church gatherings:

> *These words spake Jesus, and lifted up his eyes to
> heaven, and said, Father, the hour is come; glorify thy
> Son, that thy Son also may glorify thee: As thou hast
> given him power over all flesh, that he should give eternal
> life to as many as thou hast given him. And this is life
> eternal, that they might know thee the only true God, and*

Jesus Christ, whom thou hast sent. I have glorified thee on the earth: I have finished the work which thou gavest me to do. And now, O Father, glorify thou me with thine own self with the glory which I had with thee before the world was.

I have manifested thy name unto the men which thou gavest me out of the world: thine they were, and thou gavest them me; and they have kept thy word. Now they have known that all things whatsoever thou hast given me are of thee. For I have given unto them the words which thou gavest me; and they have received them, and have known surely that I came out from thee, and they have believed that thou didst send me. I pray for them: I pray not for the world, but for them which thou hast given me; for they are thine. And all mine are thine, and thine are mine; and I am glorified in them.

And now I am no more in the world, but these are in the world, and I come to thee. Holy Father, keep through thine own name those whom thou hast given me, that they may be one, as we are. While I was with them in the world, I kept them in thy name: those that thou gavest me I have kept, and none of them is lost, but the son of perdition; that the scripture might be fulfilled. And now come I to thee; and these things I speak in the world, that they might have my joy fulfilled in themselves. I have given them thy word; and the world hath hated them, because they are not of the world, even as I am not of the world. I pray not that thou shouldest take them out of the world, but that thou shouldest keep them from the evil. They are not of the world, even as I am not of the world.

Sanctify them through thy truth: thy word is truth. As thou hast sent me into the world, even so have I also sent them into the world. And for their sakes I sanctify myself, that they also might be sanctified through the truth.

Neither pray I for these alone, but for them also which shall believe on me through their word; That they all may be one; as thou, Father, art in me, and I in thee, that they also may be one in us: that the world may believe that thou hast sent me. And the glory which thou gavest me I have given them; that they may be one, even as we are one: I in them, and thou in me, that they may be made perfect in one; and that the world may know that thou hast sent me, and hast loved them, as thou hast loved me.

Father, I will that they also, whom thou hast given me, be with me where I am; that they may behold my glory, which thou hast given me: for thou lovedst me before the foundation of the world. O righteous Father, the world hath not known thee: but I have known thee, and these have known that thou hast sent me. And I have declared unto them thy name, and will declare it: that the love wherewith thou hast loved me may be in them, and I in them, (John 17:1-26)

In studying this passage I have found nine particular prayers of Jesus (which are discussed in the following chapters) that have not fully come to pass in the lives of Believers today—nine petitions that appear to remain unanswered.

In this passage Jesus is praying for His disciples, but in verse 20 He says, "Neither pray I for these alone, but for them also which shall believe on me through their word." Thus Believers in all the centuries following are included in this prayer, because we are those who have believed on Christ through the word and testimony of the disciples. When Jesus prayed for his disciples in John 17, He was also praying for us.

How is it that Jesus' own prayers might yet be unfulfilled? Before we discuss that, let's look at what they were:

1. We would know the only true God (see John 17:3),

2. We would be one as He and His Father are one (see John 17:21),

3. We would have His joy (see John 17:13),

4. We would be kept from evil (see John 17:15),

5. We would be sanctified through the truth (see John 17:19),

6. We would behold His glory (see John 17:24),

7. We would be made perfect (see John 17:23),

8. The world would know that we have been with Jesus (see John 17:22-23, 25, and Acts 4:13), and

9. The love of God would be released to the world through us (see John 17:26).

These prayers have been partially answered from time to time and in the lives of individuals, but Jesus was praying for His Body as a whole, the Church—no, not the church on the corner, the Catholic Church, the Baptist, Methodist, Charismatic, or any other specific denomination; First Assembly, Faith Community, or whatever other individual congregation that we may belong to, but the universal Church comprised of all who have called upon the name of Jesus to be saved.

Can we with any honesty say that these prayers have been wholly answered when you look at so-called Christians today? Do we know God? Have we become one with Him? Have we been perfected? Do His joy, love and glory pour forth in our lives? You must surely admit that the Church on earth today is a far cry from the "glorious church, not having spot, or wrinkle, or any such thing" (Ephesians 5:27) for which He plans to return. Could it be that we, His Body on earth, have failed to understand and fulfill His will for our lives?

While studying these prayers, I have come to realize that it is a case of the latter—they cannot be answered without our cooperation. Because of God's gift of free will in our lives, we have failed to allow His desires for us to take precedence over our own will.

Perhaps the best example of this is that it is God's will for all to be saved (see I Timothy 2:3-4), but are all then automatically saved? No! We must make our own choice to accept Jesus as Lord and Savior. It is with our mouth that we must confess Jesus as Lord and with our heart that we believe God raised Him from the dead in order to be saved (see Romans 10:9-10). Your father can't do that for you; your mother can't do that for you, and even God Himself won't do that for you. We have the choice of whether or not to connect with what God has already provided. It is just as if I went to the store and bought a present for my wife, and took it home and gave it to her. Though it is bought and paid for and truly belongs to her, she will never be able to use it until she decides to unwrap the box and accept the gift!

So it is with God's will for our lives. Jesus paid the price for our total salvation through His death on the Cross. Unless you and I are willing to receive His gift, it is forever lost to us. No matter how much our hearts cry out to have His will accomplished in our lives, we must first receive His gift of salvation according to His Word.

When I first realized all of this, I suddenly began to better understand the dissatisfaction I had expressed in my professor's office. My heart was crying out for God's will in my life; my spirit was expressing dissatisfaction in conforming to the world's way of living and thinking about how one should become a Believer. My heart told me that there had to be something more.

Then when I recognized that not all Christ's prayers had been completely answered and that if I would make myself available to Him I could be instrumental in their being fulfilled, I received a sense of destiny that gave my life purpose and meaning. Suddenly Divine truth penetrated the core of my being and my life mattered! The purpose for my life—and for the life of every Christian on this earth—is to stand in agreement with our Lord and Savior for his prayers to be fully answered, just as I stood in agreement with His will for me to be saved.

It was as if a giant vacuum had begun to remove the dross from my life—the clouds of confusion vanished from my mind, and the burdensome oughts and shoulds fell off my shoulders. All I had to do was pray in agreement with Christ, walk in agreement with His Spirit, and then see His prayers answered in the world around me! When Believers come together in what we traditionally call Church with a desire to see His prayers answered, it is at that point where heaven and earth meet, where the mind of Christ can be revealed, and His power made manifest.

This is the answer to every person's identity, destiny, inferiority, or insecurity. We have no purpose, we have no meaning, and our destiny is unsecured because Christ's prayers are not yet completely answered! All we have to do is pay attention to His prayers and be obedient to His direction regarding how to fulfill them!

JESUS WANTS YOU!

The disciples did have an advantage: They had been with Jesus and seen His Father's will work through Him everyday for three years. When He left them, and they received the Holy Spirit on the day of Pentecost, they had a living example of how to operate in what they had received. Yet, in truth, the greatest among them had never experienced any of that!

The Apostle Paul had never followed Jesus around the towns and villages of Israel watching Him heal the sick, cast out demons, and raise the dead. Perhaps that is why he left us the most explicit instructions for living the Christian life. He wrote more epistles that became part of the New Testament than any other. I have little doubt that he also read the Gospels about Jesus more diligently than any of the rest because they had experienced these stories first-hand. We certainly don't have the advantage that the disciples had of walking with Jesus, but we do have the same resources, and more, than Paul had. He simply read what the others had written and then believed and walked in as much—if not more—of the power of God as had the disciples.

It is time for us to do the same. We need to read what these men of God wrote about Jesus and simply believe it, rejecting whatever others may have told us we are to expect. God will not contradict His Word, but He will confirm it with signs. (See Mark 16:20.)

It is time for us to pay attention to the prayers Jesus prayed for us.

CHAPTER THREE

⤜ ⤛

Jesus, My Lord
and My Friend

*. . . that they might know the only true God,
and Jesus Christ, whom thou hast sent.*

JOHN 17:3

MY PRAYER IN JERUSALEM on February 17, 1993 was, "God, I'm hungry. I want to know You. Will You use me?"

The funny thing is this was not at the beginning of my Christian walk, nor even the beginning of my ministry. I was already established as a minister and was doing quite well. I had been to the White House to serve on advisory boards comprised of ministers. I had been a guest on national television and radio talk shows. I was speaking regularly at churches and events, and met often with world leaders. *My* ministry was doing fine. The problem was that I no longer wanted to do *my* ministry; I wanted to do *Jesus'* ministry.

I had come to realize that I knew a lot *about* Jesus and could talk about Him for hours, but *I didn't really know Him.* Here I was trying to serve Jesus with all of *my* mind and *my* strength, and I was failing because *I didn't really even know Him!* I was desperate to change that—and as He always does, God began to answer my desperate prayers.

DO WE *KNOW* JESUS, OR ONLY KNOW *ABOUT* HIM?

In John 17:3, Jesus prayed that we "might know the only true God, and Jesus Christ, whom thou hast sent." Yet most Christians today seem content to go through life with what they or someone else *thinks* about God rather than truly *knowing* Him for themselves. The truth of the matter is, most of us are content to go to church and hear about God, His Son, and His Holy Spirit, but if He were ever to ask us to meet with Him personally, we would be too terrified to comply!

When Israel had been led forth from Egypt by Moses, had been saved by passing through the Red Sea, and had seen God's miraculous provision of manna, quail, and water from a rock in the desert, you would think that they knew God well—*but in fact they still refused to draw near to Him*. Even though they had seen Moses climb the mountain and return unharmed, his face glowing with the glory of the Lord, they chose to have someone else stand between them and God at all times because they feared knowing God personally. Moses recorded it this way:

> *And it came to pass, when ye heard the voice out of the midst of the darkness, (for the mountain did burn with fire,) that ye came near unto me, even all the heads of your tribes, and your elders; And ye said, Behold, the LORD our God hath shewed us his glory and his greatness, and we*

*have heard his voice out of the midst of the fire: we have
seen this day that God doth talk with man, and he liveth.*

*Now therefore why should we die? for this great fire will
consume us: if we hear the voice of the LORD our God any
more, then we shall die. For who is there of all flesh, that
hath heard the voice of the living God speaking out of the
midst of the fire, as we have, and lived? Go thou near, and
hear all that the LORD our God shall say: and speak thou
unto us all that the LORD our God shall speak unto thee;
and we will hear it, and do it,* (Deuteronomy 5:23-27.)

In other words, though they knew *of* God's greatness, His miracle-working power to deliver, and had heard Him speak from the
cloud that had descended upon the mountaintop, they did not want
to get too close to Him because of fear. They said, "Go *thou* near"—in
other words, "Moses, you go and talk to God. You find out His plans.
Then come and tell us. We will do whatever He wants, but we just
don't want to have to get that close to Him."

Are we really any different today? We flock to churches to do
what? Hear from God? Heavens no! We flock to church to hear others
tell us what *they* have learned about God. "Well, my pastor says . . ."
or "Such and such minister said the other day . . ." or "I read in a
certain book this past week . . ." But take time to get on our knees
and enter the Holy of Holies for ourselves? Get our instructions from
God first hand? Draw near and get to know God and his nature for
ourselves? Can you and I really cast aside our fear and do that?

Don't misunderstand, learning from pastors, teachers, traveling
evangelists, and elders in the church is important, but are you adding
their teachings to the knowledge of God you have attained through

time spent with Him? Or, are they your sole source for learning about God?

One of our biggest hindrances to knowing God is that we don't really believe we *can* know Him. Think about it. The Bible is filled with promises by God to *know* Him if we are just willing to draw near, but do you know God even as well as some of your acquaintances? Is He the first One you go to for advice, to share your financial needs, or to spend leisure time? How well do we—any of us— really know God?

JESUS CAME TO A PEOPLE WHO NO LONGER KNEW GOD

When Jesus began His ministry, He was constantly confronted by religious leaders to whom the same Old Testament offers to know God had been made. But they chose rather to live within the confines of the Law rather than drawing near to Him through His Son, Jesus Christ. They spent more time attempting to make His Word harsh and unforgiving than in studying the Scriptures. They spent no time with God individually or corporately, and much time in perfecting the art of religion for show. They sat and listened to men debate their own opinions about God until they were so far removed from His heart that they were ready to condemn God in the person of Jesus as a heretic and a blasphemer when He offered truth to them! Think about it! Throughout history how many have been condemned by the Church itself as heretics when in fact they were diligently trying to lead people back to true worship, true religion, and a true relationship with God?

When Jesus returns for His Bride, the Church, will He find that His betrothed doesn't know Him?

God forbid! Instead the Scriptures say:

Christ also loved the church, and gave himself for it;
That he might sanctify and cleanse it with the washing
of water by the word, That he might present it to himself
a glorious church, not having spot, or wrinkle, or any
such thing; but that it should be holy and without blem-
ish, (Ephesians 5:24-27.)

Could this possibly be a church that knows Him as little as we do today?

CAN YOU AND I BE "FRIENDS" WITH GOD?

God has always revealed Himself to those who truly desire to know Him—and such were called the friends of God.

The Bible says of Abraham:

Abraham believed God, and it was imputed unto him
for righteousness: and he was called the Friend of God,
(James 2:23.)

Art not thou our God, who didst drive out the inhabit-
ants of this land before thy people Israel, and gavest it to
the seed of Abraham thy friend forever? (II Chronicles
20:7.)

Why was he called God's friend? Abraham was a man who communicated with God directly, making a covenant with him through the blood sacrifice of animals (see Genesis 15:7-17) and circumcision (see Genesis 17:1-14), pleading for the people of Sodom and Gomorrah (see Genesis 18:22-33), and obedient even to the death of his own son (see Genesis 22:1-18). He was a man who knew God through direct contact with Him and became the father of two covenants, both the Old Covenant to the Jews and the New Covenant, because his willingness to sacrifice His own son for God was the precursor of God's willingness to sacrifice *His* own Son for humankind. Abraham knew God through a one-on-One relationship where there was mutual respect and dedication—Abraham knew God personally by spending time with Him continually.

Look what the Bible says of Jacob, the man who wrestled with God until he received His blessing:

> *And he [God] said, Thy name shall be called no more Jacob, but Israel: for as a prince hast thou power with God and with men, and hast prevailed. . . . And Jacob called the name of the place Peniel: for I have seen God face to face, and my life is preserved,* (Genesis 32:28, 30 [insert added].)

It was through coming face-to-face with God that Jacob came to know Him and have power with God and men.

Look at what the Bible says about Moses:

> *And the* LORD *spake unto Moses face to face, as a man speaketh unto his friend,* (Exodus 33:11.)

Why was this? Look at the desires of Moses' heart as expressed in this prayer that appears just a few verses later:

> *I pray thee, if I have found grace in thy sight, show me now thy way, that I may know thee, that I may find grace in thy sight: and consider that this nation is thy*

people. . . . If thy presence go not with me, carry us not up hence. For wherein shall it be known here that I and thy people have found grace in thy sight? is it not in that thou goest with us? so shall we be separated, I and thy people, from all the people that are upon the face of the earth. . . . I beseech thee, show me thy glory, (Exodus 33:13, 15-16, 18 .)

According to *Vine's Complete Expository Dictionary of Old and New Testament Words,* "'To know' God is to have an intimate experiential knowledge of Him."[1] Again, Moses knew God because he had experienced Him personally.

Many think that knowing God is the privilege of a chosen few—those selected from each generation—Abraham, Moses, David, Paul. Yet even these were not selected by God so much as they simply made themselves available to Him. These were men who waited on God, spent tremendous time alone in prayer with Him, men whose hearts desired nothing else but to know God. And it has always been people like these men with such uncompromisingly desperate hearts to whom God has revealed Himself.

GETTING TO KNOW HIM

If you really desire to know Jesus, it is not much different than getting acquainted with another person. If one wanted to get to know a famous person, for example, the first step would be to read their biography or research them on the Internet. The biography of Jesus is widely available in numerous versions of the Gospel. The accounts of those who walked with Jesus are included, as are those of the Apostle Paul in Acts, the various epistles, and letters from John, Peter, and Jude. As in getting to know another person, the best way to become familiar with Jesus is to spend time talking with Him, and listen carefully to what He has to say through His Word. In Matthew 11:28-29 Jesus said to His disciples:

> *Come unto me, all ye that labour and are heavy laden, and I will give you rest. Take my yoke upon you, and learn of me; for I am meek and lowly in heart: and ye shall find rest unto your souls.*

This is the opportunity we have through prayer; we can talk with Him in a quiet place, and get to know His heart by listening with spiritual ears.

However, if we come to that meeting with preconceived notions and do all the talking ourselves, we know no more about that person when we leave than when we arrived. If we are truly going to *know* Him, then we must set aside any preconceived notions and come to Him ready and willing to learn. We can learn to recognize and discern His voice more clearly and then compare what we hear during times spent in His Word; He will never contradict Himself. As He said in John 10:

> *He who enters by the door is a shepherd of the sheep. To him the doorkeeper opens, and the sheep hear his voice, and he calls his own sheep by name and leads them out. When he puts forth all his own, he goes ahead of them, and the sheep follow him because they know his voice. . . .“I am the good shepherd,”* (John 10:2-4, 11 NASB.)

Notice that the sheep have learned the voice of the shepherd because they have lived closely with him for some time. The shepherd does not just drop by once a week to spend an hour or so with the sheep; the animals make their way by following the shepherd. They go where he leads and nowhere else. They don't choose a field and then try to convince the shepherd to come there; they only eat from the fields and drink from the streams where he leads them:

> *The Lord is my shepherd; I shall not want. He maketh me to lie down in green pastures: he leadeth me beside the still waters. 3 He restoreth my soul: he leadeth me in the paths of righteousness for his name's sake,* (Psalm 23:1-3, KJV.)

It is time to really get to know God, not to just know about Him. Sincere Believers can impede what God is trying to do on the earth today because they are content to be Christians outwardly all the while continuing to follow their own inward desires. (See I Corinthians 3:1-3.) The same thing that happened to the religious people in the time of Jesus is what is happening today: We follow God through a prescribed list of do's and don'ts as opposed to having a living relationship with the Holy God. Think about this for a moment.

There was a time I would have scoffed at the thought that I was living by a list of rules rather than following Christ personally. I discovered that my actions were more dictated by trying to impress others with my so-called Christianity than by having the same priorities as God.

In the 1980s, I was intoxicated with power and had no idea how deceived I was in my fleshly pursuits. During the early days of the Reagan era, I was on the VIP list, and was invited time and again to the White House. Oh my, I had arrived! One day I would have lunch with the President of the United States or a member of his Cabinet, in the company of other religious leaders. Another time, I might be in a special briefing with Secretary of State Robert McFarland, challenging him concerning the Word of God.

I was also once asked to briefly address the Republican National Convention when it met in Dallas, Texas, for a special session. Following that, I was invited to a reception with the President's Cabinet and some of the most powerful people in the world. Man, was I smoking! But one day as I was having lunch in the White House with the President and members of his Cabinet, the stench of my flesh wafted up and hit me in the face. I was sitting next to Charles Colson, former Special Counsel to President Richard Nixon. He had been imprisoned following the Watergate Scandal.

"Chuck," I said, "have you been back since Watergate?"

"No," he said, "this is my first time."

"You must be happy about these strategies under discussion, especially since you had a lot to do with them."

"No, it's the last thing on my mind," he said. "I just felt the Lord wanted me to come, but what I'm really excited about is going to visit death row inmates tonight to share the Gospel."

Looking at Chuck, I saw such brokenness and humility. He was anticipating his appointment with Jesus that night at the death house, not the White House. Yet many of us in that room were pushing and shoving, scheming and conniving to have our pictures taken with the President, saying a few words or slipping a note to him. Christ must surely have been weeping. The only "Who's Who" list He cares about is whose name is written in the Lamb's Book of Life.

I was so polluted and yet I was strutting like a rooster—arrogant, proud, hot-tempered, and even offended when my wife did not treat me like royalty. Didn't she realize that I'm a man of God and a very, very important one at that? What a stench in the nostrils of God!

CHAPTER FOUR

✦ ✦

What Is a Christian Without Christ?

"I am the vine, you are the branches.
He who abides in Me, and I in him, bears much
fruit; for without Me you can do nothing."

JOHN 15:55, NKJV

WE MAY BE MORAL, support a conservative political agenda, and enroll our children in Christian schools, yet still be a million miles from the heart of God. Our church may preach repentance as did John the Baptist with hundreds responding nightly, or we may be famous in Christian circles, drunk on our ambitions rather than seeking His heart for a lost and dying world, yet blind to the Person of Jesus Christ. We are obsessed with our own slogans and bask in the world's accolades. As the kingdoms we build (supposedly in His name) exhaust us, we promise Him that one day—when we have the time—we will hotly pursue Him and Him alone.

If we don't realize that Jesus is very active on the earth today and wants so badly to affect the world through us, then it is because we don't truly know Him nor have we discerned His heart. If we are not touching lives around us by His power, then it is because we do not understand His works and therefore cannot be a partaker of them.

If Jesus' prayer "that we would know God," has not come to pass, it is because we have not come into agreement with it by understanding that knowing God personally is possible. We must pursue Him. Only one thing is more powerful than Jesus' prayers and His sacrifice, and that is our human will. God has given us freedom of choice; we can choose to follow after Him, or go our own way.

The Israelites limited God's power in the desert through their unbelief (see Psalm 78:41), so they wandered for forty years instead of entering into the Promised Land. No matter how great was the work of Christ on the Cross, if a person rejects Him, they cannot be saved. If you and I are to touch the lives of people as did Jesus, then we must begin by coming into agreement with His prayer in John 17 and then seek to know God with all of our hearts!

What we don't know may not hurt us—but it definitely limits what God can do through us!

JESUS HAS CALLED US HIS FRIENDS

The idea of friendship has really become trivialized today because we take it so casually. If I asked what the difference is between a friend and an acquaintance, many of us would probably answer, "Well, a friend is someone I spend more time with because we enjoy doing the same things together. An acquaintance is simply someone I have only met a few times." Yet the biblical term for "friend" is grounded in covenant relationship. It expresses a bond and mutual obligation of one person to another—as in marriage: "All

I have—wealth, talent, time, and ability—is yours, and all you have—wealth, talent, time, and ability—is mine." In becoming friends in this sense, there is shared responsibility and commitment. True friendship is a bond which links purposes and resources to benefit present and future generations.

Today most of us have sung the song "Oh, What a Friend We Have in Jesus," but is it possible that Jesus is also singing something like "O what a friend I have in you?" Sure, we can count on God to help us when we need Him; but is this a reciprocal relationship? Is the mission of Jesus tied to our daily lives? Are we as aware of His interests half as much as we expect Him to be conscious of ours? Certainly we have seen His power and goodness at work on our behalf in our Christian lives, but if we really want to see His power at work, shouldn't we be involved with what He is trying to accomplish on the earth today? Doesn't it seem logical that this is where *greater works* come into play? Yet how are we ever going to better know what He wants to do on this earth if we aren't willing to draw close enough to Him to know His purposes?

On the same night Jesus prayed the prayer recorded in John 17, he said another incredible thing to his disciples:

> *This is my commandment, That ye love one another,*
> *as I have loved you. Greater love hath no man than this,*
> *that a man lay down his life for his friends. Ye are my*
> *friends, if ye do whatsoever I command you. Henceforth*
> *I call you not servants; for the servant knoweth not what*
> *his lord doeth: but I have called you friends; for all things*
> *that I have heard of my Father I have made known unto*
> *you. Ye have not chosen me, but I have chosen you, and*
> *ordained you, that ye should go and bring forth fruit,*

and that your fruit should remain: that whatsoever ye
shall ask of the Father in my name, he may give it you.
These things I command you, that ye love one another,
(John 15:12-17.)

If Jesus' greatest commandment was that we love our neighbors as ourselves, then I am sure some Christians would agree with a hardy, "Amen!" After all, when Jesus was asked what the greatest commandment was, this was His answer. But look at this passage again. Who was asking Him that question? It came from old covenant Believers who were under the law. Jesus' answer was that loving God with all your heart, soul, and mind and loving your neighbor as yourself were the great commandments—"On these two commandments hang all the law and the prophets," (Matthew 22:40.) But I believe that for those of us under grace—no longer under the law and the prophets—His greatest commandment in this passage is not that you "love your neighbor as yourself," but "that you love one another, *as Jesus has loved you."*

Now, let me ask you, how can we possibly love a sick person as Jesus loved a sick person, if we do not exercise the power available to us to see that person healed? How can we love a mentally ill person or someone possessed of a devil, if we do not have the supernatural knowledge to deliver them from the thing oppressing them? How can we possibly love a person in prison, on the street, someone who is poor and hungry, or someone who has just lost their home with the same love with which Jesus loved, if we do not have the power to multiply resources to help them as Jesus did with the little boy's lunch of a fish and two loaves used to feed the five thousand? Can Jesus honestly expect us to love the world as He did if we do not have the power to do the things He did? Obviously He didn't expect us to love like He did without His miracle-working power, because it was earlier that night when He also said, "He that believeth on me, the works that I do shall he do also; and greater works than these shall he do; because I go unto my Father," (John 14:12.)

Again, this is exactly what He meant when He called us His friends. He was in essence saying, "If you make all that you have available for My purposes on the earth through your obedience, then I will make all that I have available to you to see those purposes fulfilled." He also said, "If you were just my servants, you wouldn't know what I want to accomplish on earth; but since you are my friends, I will reveal to you the will of My Father in everything and if you ask My Father anything in My Name, then He will give it to you. These things I have commanded *that you may love the world with the love with which I have loved you."*

Paul described this New Testament relationship as well:

> *God showed his great love for us by sending Christ to die for us while we were still sinners. And since we have been made right in God's sight by the blood of Christ, he will certainly save us from God's judgment. For since we were restored to friendship with God by the death of his Son while we were still his enemies, we will certainly be delivered from eternal punishment by his life. So now we can rejoice in our wonderful new relationship with God—all because of what our Lord Jesus Christ has done for us in making us friends of God.* (Romans 5:8-11 NLT.)

How well do you know this Jesus who has called you to be His friend?

During the Persian Gulf War, God sent me to Dhahran, Saudi

Arabia. One morning as I prayed, Jesus gave me directions to go to a specific hotel. He said softly to me, "The first man you see, I want you to shake his hand and ask, 'May I go with you?'"

Obediently, I followed those directions, shaking the hand of an Arab man whom I'd never met. Angrily he spat out, "Who are you?"

"May I go with you?" I asked.

"Who are you?" he asked again.

I repeated, "May I go with you?"

He complained of being in a bad mood, and then suddenly said, "Yes, be here at 5:45 tomorrow morning."

I left with no idea who he was or where we might be going. The following morning I was amazed when a dozen jeeps drove up in front of the hotel. Sitting in the fourth jeep was a four-star general who I later discovered was Mohammed Kaleed, the man whose hand I had shaken. When he saw my Bible he asked, "Are you a Christian?" I told him I was a minister.

"We behead ministers every Thursday," he quipped, "Would you like to go there with me, too?"

"I'm busy Thursday," I replied.

He laughed. "I like you."

Here I was laughing with a man who had just threatened to behead me! Could it have been anything other than the love of Christ?

Our destination took us near the border of Kuwait to meet with the Syrian high command and the Egyptian Third Army where they shared strategic invasion operations. He thought I had known what he was doing so he kept no secrets. I knew nothing, but Jesus knew everything. I was able to share the Gospel with him and other military personnel on that trip. It was definitely a miraculous opportunity, but when I left I thought that was all it was about.

Several years later after that trip to the Persian Gulf, I preached in a crusade in the Philippines. A trio of Filipino pastors greeted me warmly after the meeting, and even began to cry. I didn't think I'd preached well enough to bring pastors to tears, so I asked them why they were crying. They told me they had been in jail in Dhahran—condemned to be beheaded for preaching the Gospel. That one day, their jail cells were opened and Prince Mohammed Kaleed announced that they were free to leave. The men were weeping because they knew what I'd never known—they believed that my witness to the prince had saved their lives.

This is how Christ wants to live His life through us every day; this is what Jesus is praying for us at the right hand of the Father. He wants us to know God's will and walk in that knowledge every day. He longs for unbroken fellowship, but on His terms. He desires to reveal to the world the fullness of His glory. He is able to do "exceeding abundantly above all that we ask or think" (see Ephesians 3:20) if we just come into agreement with Him.

ARE WE ALL THAT WE CAN BE?

In these last days I believe there will be a new move in the Body of Christ where people will no longer follow a person, a denomination, a revival, or a movement, or anything originated by man, but they will follow after God. They will come together as an army receiving its orders directly from their Commanding Officer. Thus the Body will be molded together to do His works and preach His Word. It will not be caught up with ego and self-sufficiency or concerned with who gets the glory or the financial reward. Its desire will be the same as that of Jesus—"to do the will of Him that sent me, and to finish His work." (See John 4:34.)

Jesus longs to be known today by His children. Those who know Him should carry a sense of destiny about them. Sadly, this is untrue of many Christians today. We have no sense of destiny, little sense of purpose, and are indistinguishable from those who seek little else but their own selfish desires. When was the last time someone hungry for God walked up to you and said, "There is something about you . . . I can't place it! You have such peace. You seem so happy. What is your secret?" How often have you had such an opportunity to share about your Lord and Savior?

Those who know Jesus and spend real time with Him do have such things happen to them! I have had people with whom I have shaken hands once, ring my doorbell in the middle of the night asking me to tell them about the God they are seeking. I have been with other ministers when people have dropped to their knees, acknowledging their sin and asking how they might receive God's forgiveness. When you meet such people you are instantly humbled as you see Jesus in their eyes. You know they have been with Jesus! You know that they really know Him!

Why don't we all know Jesus in this way?

➤ ◄

CHAPTER FIVE

The Weakest Link

. . . that they may be one: as thou, Father, art in me,
and I also in thee, that they also may be one in us.

JOHN 17:21

JUST BEFORE SPEAKING at an international ministers'
conference in Wales, I read Hebrews 1:7: "And of the angels he saith,
Who maketh his angels spirits, and his ministers a flame of fire."

Immediately Jesus softly whispered to my spirit, "Ask them, 'Are
you one?' and sit down."

I wondered at this for only a moment, but when I was called
upon to speak, I simple did what Jesus had told me to do. I walked up
to the podium, asked, "Are you one?" and then returned to my seat.

Never have I seen such glory fall as the power of God fell upon
those in that place and all without anyone saying another word. The
Holy Spirit took over the meeting to such a degree that at one o'clock
the following morning, executives of the denomination were still
caught up in glory. The certificates for those who were to be ordained
that night were placed on their chests as they lay on the ground like
dead men. They could not stand in the presence of a Holy God.

With this I had a revelation of the importance God puts on unity in His Body.

DIVISION IN THE RANKS OF GOD'S ARMY

The second prayer that Jesus prayed is found in John 17:11: "that they may be one as we are one," or, in other words, that we would be one with each other in the same way that Jesus and His Father are one. That is a close relationship.

Yet according to a recent edition of the *World Christian Encyclopedia*, there are now nearly 34,000 denominations and para-denominations calling themselves Christians.[2] How can we have one God, one Bible, and one Body of Christ, yet build so many walls between us?

The answer is relatively simple: Self on the throne. The weakest link in the universal Body of Christ is not between one church and another or brother and brother, *but between us individually and Jesus Himself.* It concerns what we want to do for God and what God is actually trying to do through each of us. In our own fleshly pride, we have built kingdoms in His name, but for our own purposes. Or we have taken sincere moves of God under true Christian men and women and turned them into organizations that eventually have little, if anything, to do with what God had originally planned through their founders. This struggle has gone on in the Church since the first split. We separate from one another by majoring in the minor doctrines and our own desires instead of concentrating on being like Jesus.

WHO IS ON THE THRONE OF YOUR LIFE?

In the 1960s, a little pamphlet came out called "The Four Spiritual Laws."[3] Perhaps you have read it. One of the most remarkable things

I remember about it was the little circle diagram used to represent the world of an individual and their interests. It has always struck me as a very clear illustration of what happens in our lives with and without Jesus.

At the center of the circle was a little chair representing who, or what, ruled the life of the individual. The little book called it "the throne of your life." Whoever sat in it directed all the events of that person's life. The circle representing Self on the throne had an "S" on the chair and showed all the little circles or dots representing the things in one's life creating utter chaos. The circle indicating Jesus on the throne of our lives had a cross on the chair with all of the little circles or dots having straight lines radiating out from the center like rays emanating from the sun as in a child's drawing.

The booklet said we have a choice: We can either have Self occupying the throne of our lives and suffer from the chaos that follows, or we can allow Christ to have His rightful place on the throne of our lives and let His wisdom and guidance direct our path. That choice is then made day-by-day and moment-by-moment. The pamphlet was designed to bring nonbelievers to Christ.

Paul, however, addressed the same issue with the Christians in Corinth. Here were Spirit-filled Believers who walked as if they were unsaved—following their fleshly desires and causing divisions and strife in the Corinthian church. (See I Corinthians 3:3.) Despite having confessed Jesus as their Lord, they chose to keep Self on the throne. Because of this choice and despite the fact that the testimony of Christ was confirmed in the Believers in Corinth, they felt they had no gifts of the Spirit (see I Corinthians 1:6-7.) Effectiveness in transforming their community was extremely limited.

The Galatians had a similar problem, only they weren't giving in to their fleshly desires. Rather they were attempting to perfect themselves in Christ by reverting to the traditions and regulations of Judaism from which Christ had freed them. They were choosing to walk by flesh in setting up rules and laws to control themselves, instead of simply following the leadership of His Spirit. Paul cautioned them:

> *You foolish Galatians, who has bewitched you, before whose eyes Jesus Christ was publicly portrayed as crucified? This is the only thing I want to find out from you: did you receive the Spirit by the works of the Law, or by hearing with faith? Are you so foolish? Having begun by the Spirit, are you now being perfected by the flesh? . . . So then, does He who provides you with the Spirit and works miracles among you, do it by the works of the Law, or by hearing with faith?* (Galatians 3:1-3, 5 NASB)

Paul also had a similar word for the Colossians:

> *If you have died with Christ to the elementary principles of the world, why, as if you were living in the world, do you submit yourself to decrees, such as, "Do not handle, do not taste, do not touch!" (which all refer to things destined to perish with use)—in accordance with the commandments and teachings of men? These are matters which have, to be sure, the appearance of wisdom in self-made religion and self-abasement and severe treatment of the body, but are of no value against fleshly indulgence,* (Colossians 2:20-23 NASB.)

In other words, if you have been born again through the Holy

Spirit of God, why is it that you are trying to live in God's righteousness through the rules and religion of men and denominations rather than living by the law of love and following the leadership of the Holy Spirit? No wonder you no longer walk in God's miracle power; you have forsaken His present-day ministry either for your own fleshly desires or to build your own kingdoms—your own ministries—by using His name! No wonder you can't even get along with each other!

Don't get me wrong, there are some doctrines that separate Christian groups from non-Christian groups; there are basic tenets of faith that are evident in the Bible. We cannot forsake these and still be Believers. But, as a whole, those who call themselves Christians and divide themselves into various denominations from others who also call Jesus Lord aren't so much wrong about the basic tenets of faith—they simply don't know God. Those who don't know someone or something well often reach wrong conclusions—it is only natural. Yet because of this, most of our reasons for division and strife would disappear if we just spent ten minutes in the presence of Jesus and understood what it truly means to surrender the throne of our lives to Him.

These are the two extremes of having Self on the throne: 1) Living by selfish or fleshly desires; or 2) Living by religious tenets created by Man to define holiness. Though option two seems much more acceptable, it is just as much a form of self-worship as option one, and just as debilitating to what God wants to do on the earth today. These people think they know God, but are actually about a million miles away from *really* knowing Him. Where Self rules, there is little if any room for the acts of the Holy Spirit and God's miracle-working power. We have to make the choice: Will we live by the flesh (Self) or the Spirit? (See Romans 8:1-9.)

Life in the Spirit is the only path toward oneness with God.

THE LORD OUR GOD IS ONE
LORD WITH ONE BODY

The Oneness of God is one of the key themes throughout the Old Testament and resounds in the Shema: *Sh'ma Yis'ra'eil Adonai Eloheinu Adonai echad:* "Hear, Israel, the Lord is our God, the Lord is One." Jesus echoes this when asked about the great, or first, commandment:

> *And one of the scribes came, and . . . asked him, Which is the first commandment of all? And Jesus answered him, The first of all the commandments is, Hear, O Israel; The Lord our God is one Lord: And thou shalt love the Lord thy God with all thy heart, and with all thy soul, and with all thy mind, and with all thy strength: this is the first commandment,* (Mark 12:28-30.)

How could God's oneness breed various sects or groups to follow Him? Paul expressed concern about this same question in Ephesians:

> *With all lowliness and meekness, with longsuffering, forbearing one another in love; Endeavoring to keep the unity of the Spirit in the bond of peace. There is one body, and one Spirit, even as ye are called in one hope of your calling; One Lord, one faith, one baptism, One God and Father of all, who is above all, and through all, and in you all,* (Ephesians 4:2-6.)

Another way of saying this might be, "If all of these things are one: One God and Father of all, one Lord, one faith, one baptism, one Spirit, then there should be only one Body following Him. If we support one another in love and walk in humility, then this unity will be preserved in a bond of peace." Paul must have seen that even though the Church was only one organization at that time, division and strife within the Body were already threatening the work God had called it to do.

Paul echoed this in his letter to the Philippians:

> *If there be therefore any consolation in Christ, if any comfort of love, if any fellowship of the Spirit, if any bowels and mercies, Fulfill ye my joy, that ye be likeminded, having the same love, being of one accord, of one mind. Let nothing be done through strife or vainglory; but in lowliness of mind let each esteem others better than themselves,* (Philippians 2:1-3.)

Paul must have been well acquainted with the divisions occurring among the Jews. The Jewish people to whom Jesus came were already divided into several sects long before He was born. The groups employed different interpretations of the Scriptures: Pharisees, Sadducees, scribes, and so forth.

Did Jesus single any one of these groups out and say, "Now, you Sadducees, let me show you where the Pharisees are right and you have missed it"? No, he simply grouped them all together as a people who needed God and whose traditions had made the Word of God ineffective in their lives.

> *Why do ye also transgress the commandment of God by your tradition? . . . Ye made the commandment of God of none effect by your tradition. Ye hypocrites, well did Isaiah prophesy of you, saying, This people draweth nigh unto me with their mouth, and honoreth me with their*

lips; but their heart is far from me. But in vain they do worship me, teaching for doctrines the command-ments of men. (Matthew 15:3, 6-9.)

Jesus cared little to which group they belonged; in fact, there are instances where he didn't even care if they were Jewish![4] Jesus only cared about one thing: That each person He encoun-tered knew they could have individual and direct access to God the Father. He came in order to remove the things that kept them from God so that they could easily make the choice to follow God wholeheartedly. What was it they needed? Healing? Revelation of the truth? Provision? Freedom? Jesus became an instant link between God and a person's needs wherever His ministry took Him.

Nowhere in His ministry do we hear him saying, "No, I can't do that for you. God wants you to suffer through this for a while to teach you something." He never refused a sincere heart seeking after God. What we do see however is Him asking hard questions of those who came to Him with fleshly motives—whether they be selfish or religious—and those people turning away on their own because they weren't willing to let go of their selfishness to follow Him with pure hearts. His purpose was always to bring people to the knowledge of the Gospel.

The prophet Zephaniah foretold of a people God would rescue; people who live with this purpose:

For then will I turn to the people a pure language, that they may all call upon the name of the LORD, to serve him with one consent, (Zephaniah 3:9.)

The Hebrew here for "with one consent" is *shâkem 'echad* or literally, with one shoulder. To me, this elicits the image of several people trying to move a large boulder by putting their shoulders together as one to move it out of the way. This is God's image for how His Church should operate—all of us putting our shoulders to the things that keep others from seeing God clearly and tossing these obstacles out of the way through a unified effort. This may sound difficult, until we realize that the shoulder next to ours belongs to Jesus. The problem is that most of us never put our shoulder to the boulder with Him, because we are caught up in other endeavors. We haven't come into agreement with His prayers.

> *Two are better than one; because they have a good reward for their labor. For if they fall, the one will lift up his fellow: but woe to him that is alone when he falleth; for he hath not another to help him up. Again, if two lie together, then they have heat: but how can one be warm alone? And if one prevail against him, two shall withstand him; and a threefold cord is not quickly broken,* (Ecclesiastes 4:9-12.)

When we *know* God and walk as one with Him and His purposes, we are never alone. When we come into agreement with Him and His Word, weaving ourselves together as if we were three strands of the same rope—"a threefold cord is not easily broken"—then the most amazing things can happen! All we need are hungry hearts ready to believe His Word and act upon it in His wisdom.

While still in seminary, I was sitting in the cafeteria with a friend reading my Bible. As the rain poured down outside, I came across this passage:

He was wounded for our transgressions, bruised for our iniquities, the chastisement of our peace was upon Him and by His stripes we are healed, (Isaiah 53:5.)

Billy D'Angelo, another friend, walked in at that moment. A victim of multiple sclerosis, he wore hip-high leg braces and had holes in the knees of his pants from having repeatedly fallen. Even special shoes and braces would not keep his legs steady.

"Billy, you were healed," I announced, showing him the verse.

"I've been in church all my life and I haven't been healed yet," he replied.

Another friend, Randy Van Pay, and I hustled Billy into a prayer room where we prayed for two hours, just three young men on our faces before God. Suddenly, a white cloud descended from the ceiling down the walls to where we lay on the floor. The air felt thick, and the glory of God was so strong it felt like a thousand volts of electricity. As the cloud touched Billy, his legs straightened. He threw off the braces, ran outside into a muddy field, and stood weeping. Seeing his braces gone, students started running toward him, but spun and fell into the mud under the power of the Holy Spirit. It was an incredible move of God!

Several years later I spoke at a crusade in Uganda. When I took the platform, I simply held up my Bible and said, "The Word of God is the power of God unto salvation." People by the thousands in that meeting—many of them Muslims—began to shake as if plugged into a 220-volt outlet. As I held up my Bible, they removed demonic fetishes from around their waists and their wrists and threw them into piles. They then burned the piles, denouncing the powers of darkness. Something had happened in the heavenlies, in the Spirit-realm, that brought this incredible breakthrough. The anointing came through Christ and His Word! It was astonishing.

CHAPTER SIX

The True Purpose
of the Church

*...Thy kingdom come. Thy will be done
in earth, as it is in heaven.*

MATTHEW 6:10

IN THE ENTIRE BIBLE, Jesus only taught his disciples one prayer, which we call the Lord's Prayer today. Though many of us recite it from memory in services or on occasions where various denominations gather, how often do we really think about it or expect this prayer to be answered? Look again and think about praying this prayer as if you were binding yourself with its words and with God in order to see these requests accomplished on the earth:

> *Our Father which art in heaven, Hallowed be thy name.*
>
> *Thy kingdom come. Thy will be done in earth, as it is in heaven.*
>
> *Give us this day our daily bread.*

And forgive us our debts, as we forgive our debtors.
And lead us not into temptation, but deliver us from evil:
For thine is the kingdom, and the power, and the glory,
for ever. Amen,. (Matthew 6:9-13.)

This simple and profound prayer says:

1. I worship and praise You,

2. I want Your kingdom to be realized on earth just as it is in heaven,

3. I will trust in Your provision,

4. I will forgive others as You have forgiven me,

5. Through Your strength I will resist
   temptation and avoid evil,

6. Because You are the owner of the kingdom,
   power, and glory that will last forever,

7. Amen. (Which means "so let it be."[5])

To me, everything that is wrapped up in being a Christian is in this prayer and the main purpose of being a Christian is right there at the beginning: "Thy kingdom come. They will be done on earth, as it is in heaven."

The true purpose of the Church—the Body of Christ on the earth—is simply to see His will done here as it is in heaven.

THE KINGDOM OF HEAVEN

Look for a moment at the things to which Jesus compared the kingdom of heaven:

1. A grain of mustard seed—it may start as the smallest of all things, but when it is planted and grows, it becomes a place of shelter, lodging, and protection (see Matthew 13:31-32);

2. Yeast—though it is only added to a small part of something, it will soon permeate and change everything it comes into contact with (see Matthew 13:33),

3. A hidden treasure and a pearl of great price—for the joy of having this one thing, a person would be willing to sell everything they own to possess it (see Matthew 13:44-45), and those who trust in their wealth and possessions rather than in God will have a hard time entering into it (see Mark 10:23-26.),

4. A net—which when it is cast in the sea will return full to the boat with every kind of fish (see Matthew 13:47-50),

5. A man hiring workers for his vineyard and a king inviting guests to his son's wedding—those who come to it will receive its reward whether they come early or late, and though many are invited, only those who answer that call will enjoy its benefits: "For many are called, but few are chosen." (See Matthew 20:1-16 and 22:2-14.)

Jesus admonished us to pray that His will be done on earth as in heaven. This is what the Church was meant to do—usher in His kingdom. How can we possibly fulfill this assignment if we do not truly know Him and are One with Him?

Jesus gave a simple illustration to His disciples. I think many of us tend to miss a nuance of this teaching that would help to clarify His instructions. Please carefully read the following passage:

> *At the same time came the disciples unto Jesus, saying, Who is the greatest in the kingdom of heaven?*
>
> *And Jesus called a little child unto him, and set him in the midst of them, And said, Verily I say unto you, Except ye be converted, and become as little children, ye shall not enter into the kingdom of heaven. Whosoever therefore shall humble himself as this little child, the same is greatest in the kingdom of heaven.* (Matthew 18:1-4 .)

Most of us have heard this story before, or even a sermon or two on it, and have come away with the message that we should be like little children before God if we want to enter His kingdom. We have centered on the point that we should have the attributes of children—innocence, trustfulness, simplicity—the central meaning of this passage. And this certainly is an important part of it, *but it is not the answer to the disciples' question.* Look at the passage again, and you will see Jesus' response is two-fold: 1) Except that you become *as* a little child, you shall not enter the kingdom of heaven; and 2) Whoever shall humble himself *as* a little child shall become the greatest in the kingdom of Heaven.

Jesus is being very specific here in this second point: It is not the general principle of childlikeness that will usher us into God's kingdom on earth, but there is something special about *this one child* that will teach us great things about living in God's kingdom. Was it the identity of the child? Was he a saint who would do great things in life? Was Jesus showing the disciples someone they should look to for guidance after He was gone?

The passage offers no suggestion of this. In fact, the key to Jesus' teaching is plainly in what He said: "Whosoever therefore shall humble himself as this little child . . ." The point was not in who the child was, but *in what the child did.* How did he humble himself? *He simply did what Jesus asked without question or hesitation.*

Picture the scene again: The disciples asked Jesus a question, and in response Jesus turned around and saw a little boy walking by, perhaps carrying water for his parents or on some other task. He may simply have been running down the street playing with some friends. Jesus said, "Child," catching the boy's attention, "Come here." The boy stopped what he was doing, however important his errand or however much he may have been enjoying his play, and walked obediently to Jesus. He didn't say, "Sure, Jesus, just as soon as I finish what I am doing." Nor did he say, "Aw, com 'on, can't I finish my game first?" No, he went immediately, without saying a word. Then Jesus took the boy lovingly by the shoulders and turned him to face the disciples and said, "Whosoever shall humble himself as this little child, the same is greatest in the kingdom of heaven."

This is what I have experienced again and again in my life, though more often by accident than intent. At times when I was completely dependent upon God, knowing I could do nothing in my own strength, stripped of all self-confidence, my desperate prayer would be, "God if *You* don't do it, it can't be done." Then I simply did what God told me to do in response. I often had no idea that the desperate cry of my heart was the fertile soil in which the glory of God would be manifested. Now I see clearly that those times when Jesus moved the most powerfully were when I learned to lean heavily upon Him. He has moved most powerfully when "I" moved out of the way. Jesus would show up and softly speak, and when I obeyed, I would see His will done on earth as if we were actually standing before His throne in heaven. This is receiving the kingdom of God like a child.

> *Suffer the little children to come unto me, and forbid them not: for of such is the kingdom of God. Verily I say unto you, Whosoever shall not receive the kingdom of God as a little child, he shall not enter therein,* (Mark 10:14-15.)

It is through those that have spent time with Jesus—and obey His voice—that His kingdom becomes real on the earth.

MANY PARTS; ONE PURPOSE

Please don't misunderstand what I am about to say here: I am not calling for some ecumenical movement among all those who call themselves Christians to join together into one universal, corporate church organization. I don't care any more than Jesus did if you want to call yourself a Baptist, a Methodist, a Presbyterian, a Catholic, a Charismatic, or a Slice-and-Dice-o-matic. I only want to know: Do you *know* Jesus? Have you been with Him? Are you taking part in *His* plans to bring to fruition His kingdom on the earth? Are you obeying *His* unique plan for your life? *Are you one with Him?*

If each of us would just be one with Jesus, then we would have no problem working together on the earth to usher in His kingdom, no matter what we want to call ourselves or what our function is in His plan. This is why His Church is compared to a body with many parts with all having different functions, but working together to build itself up in unity of purpose and the love of God. Look at how Paul described it in Ephesians:

> *Therefore it says, "When He ascended on high, He led captive a host of captives, And He gave gifts to men."*
>
> *. . . for the equipping of the saints for the work of service, to the building up of the body of Christ; until we all attain to the unity of the faith, and of the knowledge of the Son of God, to a mature man, to the measure of the stature which belongs to the fullness of Christ.*
>
> *As a result, we are no longer to be children, tossed here and there by waves and carried about by every wind of doctrine, by the trickery of men, by craftiness in deceitful scheming; but speaking the truth in love, we are to grow up in all aspects into Him who is the head, even Christ, from whom the whole body, being fitted and held together by what every joint supplies, according to the proper working of each individual part, causes the growth of the body for the building up of itself in love,* (Ephesians 4:8, 13-16 NASB.)

David wrote of it in this way:

> *Behold, how good and how pleasant it is for brethren to dwell together in unity! It is like the precious ointment upon the head, that ran down upon the beard, even Aaron's beard: that went down to the skirts of his garments; As the dew of Hermon, and as the dew that descended upon the mountains of Zion: for there the*

LORD *commanded the blessing, even life for evermore,*
(Psalm 133.)

According to *Vine's*, the word *together* here "emphasizes a plu-
rality in unity. In some contexts the connotation is on community
in action."[6] Here David is describing the place where brothers and
sisters work together in this kind of unity. It is the place of God's
anointing! It is a place where we are refreshed and strengthened by
God's Spirit as the dew nourishes the grass! It is the place where God
commands blessing! And it is the place where *zoe*—from the Greek
meaning the eternal, God-kind of life—flows freely![7]

Only when Self is subjugated to Christ will we be one with God—
and each other—to have this kind of unity. We will never be one by
trying to agree with each other and putting aside differences of belief
for the sake of unity alone. We are to be one as Jesus and His Father
are one. Only when Jesus is on the throne in each of our lives can we
be in tune with His purpose and be one Body on earth able to work
corporately to bring true and lasting revival. Only when Self is subjugated to Jesus will His greater works flourish as the body of Christ
grows into His fullness and carries forth His kingdom on the earth.

This is what atonement—"at-one-ment"—is all about: *We must be
one with Jesus.*

➤➤ ◄◄

CHAPTER SEVEN

Living with Jesus' Joy

. . . that they might have my joy fulfilled in themselves.

JOHN 17:13

THE DAYS MUST HAVE been dark for all of the Israelites. The city around them lay in ruins. Even as they struggled to rebuild and repair it, they carried with them the constant fear that they would be attacked again. They worked with mortar, trowel, or a stone in one hand, and a spear or sword for defense in the other. Stone by stone, they rebuilt the wall, watching the hills around them for any sign of attack. Only occasionally did they allow their watchfulness to drift to thoughts of the day when the city walls would be fully repaired and they could leave this labor for the work of rebuilding the Temple. Their hope was in a God of whom they knew very little; yet, they longed for His presence to once again dwell in their midst.

When the walls were finally completed, the people gathered on the first day of the seventh month, the beginning of the Feast of Trumpets, and the priest mounted a platform to address the crowds. There, he opened the Book. At this, the people stood. From early morning until midday he read the law that had been given through Moses. In response to hearing the Word of their Lord that had been so far removed from them during their time of exile, the people shouted praises and called out "Amen! Amen!—So be it! So be it!" They wept under the conviction that they had so freely and unknowingly violated God's laws without even realizing it. Many fell to their faces on the ground and cried out for forgiveness, their tears mixing with the dust.

At the sight of their lamentations, their leader Nehemiah rose before them and called out:

> "Don't weep on such a day as this! For today is a sacred day before the LORD your God. . . .
>
> "Go and celebrate with a feast of choice foods and sweet drinks, and share gifts of food with people who have nothing prepared. This is a sacred day before our Lord. Don't be dejected and sad, for the joy of the LORD is your strength!". . . (Nehemiah 8:9-10, NLT.)

The Scriptures also record the people's response to this:

> So the people went away to eat and drink at a festive meal, to share gifts of food, and to celebrate with great joy because they had heard God's words and understood them, (Nehemiah 8: 12 NLT.)

The next day the people rose up and began to do what they had heard and understood from God's Word. They desired that all in the region who didn't grasp it would know and understand His Law so they could each walk in it and keep His ways. (See Nehemiah 7:73-8:18.)

I am sure that many of you have read Nehemiah 8:10: "The joy of the Lord is your strength." But how many are familiar with the story behind it? In the midst of a people defeated, fearful, and trying to rebuild their nation and faith came revival and a return to the Word of God. This renewal brought guilt and tears of conviction from those who knew they had been ignorant to the truth of God's Word. All their lives, the people had called upon and reverenced His name, but knew little of His laws. It was into this atmosphere that Nehemiah spoke these often-repeated words.

Are Christians worldwide who are trying to rebuild our faith and our defenses in the face of terrorism, recession, corporate scandals, a volatile stock market, and other chaotic events that much different than those working to rebuild Jerusalem during the days of Nehemiah? If you are a person who has picked up this book and feels convicted because you have now seen from the Scriptures that it is time to really get to know God and be one with His purposes, then my word to you is the same as Nehemiah's was to the people of God in his time: "Stop your crying and rejoice! It is time to see His Word accomplished! For the joy of the Lord Jesus is your strength!"

THE JOY OF *YOUR* LORD

In John 17, the third prayer Jesus prayed for His followers was "that they might have my joy fulfilled in themselves," (John 17:13.) Imagine that! Living in the same joy in which Jesus lived while on the earth! That is an amazing prayer and a remarkable challenge to the Body of Christ. Would anyone looking at the Church today really call its members joyful? Would they even call them a happy people? The fact is that our churches are filled with discouraged, unhappy people looking for fulfillment just as I was that day in my professor's office. We are God's frozen chosen—His own pickled people—sitting in our pews and daring our ministers to make us smile. Is this the Body that has been called to live in Jesus' joy?

It is, but it is not the Body fulfilling its calling to live in His joy. Where have we missed the target? How can the Church once again become "a chosen generation, a royal priesthood, an holy nation, a peculiar people; that ye should shew forth the praises of him who hath called you out of darkness into his marvelous light," (I Peter 2:9.)

Before we can answer that we must first understand exactly what Jesus' joy was. A quick word search of the Scriptures will show some interesting aspects of joy. In the Old Testament, we see joy expressed by the people of Israel when they had been victorious in battle, when David brought the Ark of the Covenant back to Jerusalem, when Solomon was crowned king to succeed his father, and when the Temple was finally rebuilt and rededicated in the time of Ezra and Nehemiah. When Israel was delivered from Babylonian captivity, the Psalmist expressed it this way:

> *When the LORD turned again the captivity of Zion, we were like them that dream. Then was our mouth filled with laughter, and our tongue with singing: then said they among the heathen, The LORD hath done great things for them. The LORD hath done great things for us; whereof we are glad.*
>
> *Turn again our captivity, O LORD, as the streams in the south. They that sow in tears shall reap in joy. He that goeth forth and weepeth, bearing precious seed, shall doubtless come again with rejoicing, bringing his sheaves with him,* (Psalm 126:1-6.)

The book of Proverbs also tells us:

The desire accomplished is sweet to the soul, (Proverbs 13:19.)

In the New Testament, Jesus gives an example of what joy is when he is preparing his disciples for His crucifixion and resurrection:

Verily, verily, I say unto you, That ye shall weep and lament, but the world shall rejoice: and ye shall be sorrowful, but your sorrow shall be turned into joy. A woman when she is in travail hath sorrow, because her hour is come: but as soon as she is delivered of the child, she remembereth no more the anguish, for joy that a man is born into the world. And ye now therefore have sorrow: but I will see you again, and your heart shall rejoice, and your joy no man taketh from you, (John 16:20-22.)

John the Baptist gave this example:

They came to John and said to him, "Rabbi, that man who was with you on the other side of the Jordan—the one you testified about—well, he is baptizing, and everyone is going to him."

To this John replied, "A man can receive only what is given him from heaven. You yourselves can testify that I said, 'I am not the Christ but am sent ahead of him.' The bride belongs to the bridegroom. The friend who attends the bridegroom waits and listens for him, and is full of joy when he hears the bridegroom's voice. That joy is mine, and it is now complete. He must become greater; I must become less," (John 3:26-30 NIV.)

Elsewhere in the Gospels, we see joy expressed at the birth and resurrection of Jesus and with the return of the seventy after Jesus had sent them out to "Heal the sick, cleanse the lepers, raise the dead, cast out devils," (Matthew 10:8.) In the book of Acts we also see joy when many were healed in Samaria, when Peter was delivered from prison by the angel in answer to the prayers of the early Believers, and at various times during the missionary trips of Paul when Believers heard that others had received the Word of God and accepted Jesus.

If you look closely at these examples you will discover some interesting things about joy:

1. Joy comes after victory—and victory does not come without a battle or a struggle (as after a war or the birth of a child).

2. People turn from tears to joy—joy often comes after a period of sorrow or loss (as at the time of exile coming to an end). According to Vine's: "Experiences of sorrow prepare for, and enlarge, the capacity for 'joy.'"[8]

3. Joy comes when something long hoped for is finally manifested (as after the fulfillment of prophecy—such as the coming of the Messiah).

4. Joy always seems to come in connection with the will of God being done (as at the receiving of the Word of God by others after persecutions or when Israel was delivered from her seventy years of exile).

Joy, which is internal and constant, can thus be contrasted with happiness which is dependent on outward circumstances. Contentment is a state in which we choose to be satisfied for those things we already possess. Joy comes when something hoped for has been realized. The Psalmist wrote in Psalm 30:5: "weeping may endure for a night, but joy *cometh* in the morning." Our joy should be based on a constant—our relationship with God—and not on feelings.

Look at another example Jesus gave in the parable of the talents (see Matthew 25:14-30):

> *And so he that had received five talents came and brought other five talents, saying, Lord, thou deliveredst unto me five talents: behold, I have gained beside them five talents more. His lord said unto him, Well done, thou good and faithful servant: thou hast been faithful over a few things, I will make thee ruler over many things: enter thou into the joy of thy lord. He also that had received two talents came and said, Lord, thou deliveredst unto me two talents: behold, I have gained two other talents beside them. His lord said unto him, Well done, good and faithful servant; thou hast been faithful over a few things, I will make thee ruler over many things: enter thou into the joy of thy lord,* (Matthew 25:20-23.)

In this parable, Jesus likens the kingdom of God to a man who has gone away and left tasks for his servants. Those who entered into "the joy of their Lord" were those who used what He gave them to increase His kingdom and those who were reproved were those that did nothing with what they were given. *Entering into His Joy thus comes from fulfilling His tasks on the earth with what He has given us!*

This was Jesus' joy—fulfilling the will of His Father. The Bible tells us in the book of Hebrews:

> *Jesus . . . who for the joy that was set before him*
> *endured the cross, despising the shame,* (Hebrews 12:2.)

What was the joy that was set before Him? It was the manifestation of God's kingdom on the earth in the life of everyone who believed on Him.

When do we see Jesus the most joyful and satisfied in the gospels?

1. After he had spoken to the woman at the well in Samaria (John 4):

    > *I have meat to eat that ye know not of. . . . My meat is*
    > *to do the will of him that sent me, and to finish his work,*
    > (John 4:32, 34.)

2. When others showed unprecedented faith (the Roman Centurion and the Syrophoenician woman):

    > *When Jesus heard it, he marveled, and said to them*
    > *that followed, Verily I say unto you, I have not found so*
    > *great faith, no, not in Israel,* (Matthew 8:10.)

3. When the seventy returned to Him, having walked in His miraculous power:

    > *And the seventy returned again with joy, saying, Lord,*

even the devils are subject unto us through thy name....
In that hour Jesus rejoiced in spirit, (Luke 10:17, 21.)

All these were cases where the will of God was manifested on the earth. Jesus' joy was that His Father's will be done on earth as it is in heaven.

JOY IS WON . . .

So, before Jesus could know this joy in seeing God's will manifested on the earth, He had to:

1. Know God's will,

2. Align Himself with that will, and

3. Do what God had instructed Him to do through the Holy Ghost to make that will a reality.

The rest was up to God. Jesus was not concerned with whether God's will was to be manifested immediately or gradually, He only made sure He did and said those things directed by His Father. (See John 8:28, 38.)

Thus, for us as well, joy comes from knowing the will of God, aligning ourselves with it through prayer and agreement with His Word, and acting according to the leadership of His Holy Spirit. Until we truly know God, realize a sense of His purpose and mission for our lives, plug into it, and begin to walk in it, we will not know joy the same way Jesus did. While we may feel happy, be blessed and have contentment, we will never experience His true joy except in the fulfillment of God's purposes for our life or in the lives of those around us. Real joy is grounded in the fulfillment of the will of God. It comes from knowing and fulfilling the Word and will of God!

. . . BUT JOY CAN ALSO BE TAKEN BY FAITH

Thus, many of us have probably experienced at least a bit of His joy when we saw a friend saved—or when we were saved ourselves!—or when we experienced the will of God being manifested in ourselves or someone we know. But as New Testament Believers, we don't have to wait for something to happen to have joy! We can have joy when we realize that God's grace has been extended to us! When we come to realize that it is by His grace that we are saved and it is a gift freely given, then true joy takes up residence. (See Ephesians 2:8.)

If we have God's Word on something, then we can rejoice. We can rejoice in our hope of Heaven, we can rejoice that Jesus will come again, and we can rejoice that the kingdom of darkness is eternally defeated. Why? Because, like the simple song says, "for the Bible tells me so."

Thus, by faith, we can look at any circumstance, see what God has promised about it and rejoice! If we know God's will and are walking in His purposes, then we have a great deal of room for His joy, regardless of how things appear—for "faith is the substance of things hoped for, the evidence of things not seen," (Hebrews 11:1.)

It was an extremely hot July in Canada where I was preaching at a camp meeting. My birthday, June 30, happened to fall during the event. Taking a morning off, my friend Bill Fletcher and I went fishing. We found a boat on a lake with a guide named Harry who took us out. To use a biblical phrase for it, "We fished and caught nothing." Bill had been asleep for almost an hour when I finally stretched out on the deck of the boat. I lay there, praying and complaining over the time and money wasted. To make matters worse, I had to listen to Harry who, it seemed, was cursing the name of my

Lord and Savior every five minutes. While I complained, Jesus softly whispered, "I sent you here because I am going to catch a fish."

I turned my head, looked at Harry and realized what Jesus was saying. I asked the Lord to forgive my whining, sat up and began to share the Gospel with Harry. As I did, Bill woke up and prayed softly. Little did I know what was about to take place.

"Harry," I said, "you see that pole there with the line in the water? There's a hook with bait on it. Now, if a big fish took that hook and the line started playing out and you started screaming, 'set the hook,' and I did nothing, then I would never have the joy of catching that fish. Harry, you are the big fish that Jesus wants to catch today."

As I said that, the line went screeching off the reel. Harry's face turned white. "I can't believe it," he muttered, "This has to be God." Then he screamed, "Set the hook! Set the hook!"

What a joy it was for me to land an enormous trout on my birthday. Harry was astonished. He shouted repeatedly, "I can't believe it. It's the biggest rainbow trout I have ever seen in my life—must be over fourteen pounds!"

Then he said, "Pray for me, I want to receive Jesus."

I prayed for Harry and noticed precious tears filling his eyes as he experienced the living Christ. As we arrived back at the dock, his fishing buddies, whose boats had already come in, asked, "Harry, did you catch anything?"

"Oh!" he said, "two huge fish were caught today. That preacher caught the biggest rainbow I've ever seen and Jesus caught me."

CHAPTER EIGHT

➤ ◄

Walking in His Shadow

*Therefore the children of men put their trust
under the shadow of Your wings.*

PSALM 36:7, NKJV

WHEN WE LIVE OUR LIVES spending time with God to get to know Him and His purposes, opening ourselves to consider and be part of manifesting His kingdom on the earth, then we should have constant joy within, welling up and spilling out. It should be an infectious joy that makes others want to partake. It should be in us as it was in Jesus, and should attract people to us as it did to Him. Just as people should know we are Christians by our love, so should they know we are different because of our joy. If we are truly walking with Jesus, allowing Him to guide our steps, then we should be constantly experiencing the benefits of His Holy Spirit. Just as those who were healed when Peter's shadow fell across them, we should be more fully experiencing the benefits of the Holy Spirit as we follow closely behind Jesus.

But again, here is that struggle between Self and putting on Christ, between the flesh and the Spirit. Really, it is the struggle between our discontent and walking in Jesus' joy! This is why some churches are known more for hypocrisy than joy: The members are walking in the flesh rather than His Spirit!

REDEFINING "SELF"

To this point, I have equated Self with what the Bible calls flesh: The part of us tied to the sin nature we had before coming to Christ and the part of us that lives according to natural rather than spiritual things. It is worth taking a moment here to look at this thing which battles with the Spirit and keeps us from living the spiritual life every day. What is Self? What is our flesh?

The Bible tells us that people have three components—spirit, soul, and body. I also believe that in the soul rests the seat of the mind, will, and emotions. Simply put, our spirit is the part of ourselves that connects to God and is the vine through which spiritual fruit grows in our lives. If this vine is grafted into Jesus, we are very fruitful; if not, our fruit is worthless and should be cut away. (See John 15:1-8.) The flesh then is our body that touches the natural/physical world. It is the seat of our emotions, if you will, that causes us to lust after other things; it is the part of us that touches and appreciates material wealth, the part of us that interacts with the world around us. In this sense it is the seat of our sin nature because it is defined only by the created being and not the Creator. It is the part of us that would like to believe the physical world is all there is, so why not enjoy everything it has to offer without restraint! In Luke 12:16-19, Jesus, in the parable of the rich man, warned of trusting in wealth:

> *"The ground of a certain rich man yielded an abundant harvest. He thought to himself, 'What shall I do? I have no place to store my crops.' "Then he said, 'This is*

what I'll do. I will tear down my barns and build bigger ones, and there I will store my surplus grain. And I'll say to myself, "You have plenty of grain laid up for many years. Take life easy; eat, drink and be merry."'

Why should we not be gluttonous drunkards given over to the lusts of our eyes? Why not fight for our own rights and give in to our jealousies?

If ye have bitter envying and strife in your hearts, glory not, and lie not against the truth. This wisdom descendeth not from above, but is earthly, sensual (or natural), devilish. For where envying and strife is, there is confusion and every evil work, (James 3:14-16 [insert added].)

This is what the sin nature or our flesh encourages us to do: To envy, to strive with others, to be wrathful, and to walk in other works of the flesh. (See Galatians 5:19-20.)

Then, as many see it, there is the soul, caught in the middle of the flesh and the spirit, struggling to choose what is right. This is the "I" Paul talks of in Romans 7, the Self: The mind, will, and emotions of a person struggling between flesh and the spirit:

I don't understand myself at all, for I really want to do what is right, but I don't do it. Instead, I do the very thing I hate. I know perfectly well that what I am doing is wrong, and my bad conscience shows that I agree that the law is good. But I can't help myself, because it is sin inside me (my flesh) that makes me do these evil things.

I know I am rotten through and through so far as my old sinful nature (my flesh) is concerned. No matter which way I turn, I can't make myself do right. I (my soul, my will) want to, but I can't. When I want to do good, I don't. And when I try not to do wrong, I do it anyway. But if I am doing what I don't want to do, I am not really the one doing it; the sin within me (my flesh) is doing it.

It seems to be a fact of life that when I want to do what is right, I inevitably do what is wrong. I love God's law with all my heart (my spirit). But there is another law (my sin nature within my flesh) at work within me that is at war with my mind (my "self"). This law wins the fight and makes me a slave to the sin that is still within me. Oh, what a miserable person I am! Who will free me from this life that is dominated by sin? (Romans 7:15-25 NLT [inserts added].)

It is like the age-old illustration we see in so many stories: On one shoulder sits a little devil and on the other sits a little angel, in the middle is our head—our mind—trying to reason and decide what to do. Self is trying to do what is right, but is so strongly attracted to what is wrong. Is Jesus on the throne of our lives, or is sin? The choice to do what is godly seems so obvious, but the attraction to do what is wrong feels so right! It is as if there is a direct line from the spiritual through the Self to the natural—a supernatural tug-of-war. God is on one end; we, the rope, are in the middle, and Satan is on the other end, pulling in the opposite direction. There we are caught in the middle, pulled back and forth to the point that we feel we may be torn in half. What hope have we? What can we possibly do?

What we need to do is view this struggle as God might, not the way humankind has pictured it all these years. Paul did not end this discussion with "Oh, what a miserable person I am!" He ended his discourse in Romans 7:25 with "Thanks be to God, who delivers me through Jesus Christ our Lord!"

Self must be redefined. If it is our ego, as psychologists call it—that within us which influences our decisions and defines who we are, what we think, and how we act—then Self is not so much evil as it is confused. If it were simple, it would just be a matter of saying that which chooses evil is evil and that which chooses the good is good. We either obey the little devil on the one shoulder, or the little angel on the other. But the problem is we are clouded with self-doubt, lack of self-esteem, self-criticism, self-deception, self this, that, and the other! Self is truly so interwoven with ego that it tends to pay little attention to good or evil and just acts to insure its own preservation. Forget trying to listen to the advice of the little devil or the little angel; Self is just trying to survive! We rarely have the inclination to sit down and make every decision consciously! Most of the time we just act according to preconditioned thinking and patterns formed from the day we were born.

Most of us have little joy in our lives because it has very little to do with our self-concept. Self has been defined by our culture, background, and environment—wild vines into which we have joined ourselves regardless of the fruit they bear—and self-preservation is the rule of the day. Satan doesn't have to influence us to do evil or keep us from God—he just has to keep us so busy that we continue to act out of habit rather than pruning the bad and being grafted into Jesus! The devil is not the problem! We are the problem, and have yet to learn that we cannot draw vitality from anyone but Jesus! Without His vitality, how can we ever hope to resist the ever-so-attractive desires of the flesh?

Look at what Paul went on to say immediately after the thought-provoking passage we just discussed in Romans 7:25:

> *There is no condemnation for those who belong to Christ Jesus. For the power of the life-giving Spirit has freed you through Christ Jesus from the power of sin that leads to death. . . . He sent his own Son in a human body like ours, except that ours are sinful. God destroyed sin's control over us by giving his Son as a sacrifice for our sins. He did this so that the requirement of the law would be fully accomplished for us who no longer follow our sinful nature but instead follow the Spirit.* (Romans 8:1-4 NLT.)

Thus we need to change our self-concept from sin-consciousness to Christ-consciousness! We need to stop defining ourselves by our past, our culture, or our natural world. We must stop measuring ourselves by ourselves and defining *good* by looking at those around us and saying, "Well, at least I am not like that person there!" (See II Corinthians 10:12-14.) We must begin to define ourselves by the standard of Jesus. That, of course, will take some self-awareness which will only come from drawing close to Jesus and being open and vulnerable in the light of His Word until we are changed into His likeness. We must know Him, be one with Him, and then we can enter into His joy.

I believe God sees it differently. His idea is that spirit, soul, and body are but a conduit. We should be pipelines through which the Holy Spirit can manifest the kingdom of God, causing His will to be done on earth as it is in heaven. We should be drawing power, strength, and life from the Spirit. That power should be channeled through the soul, and body into the physical realm, rather than our simply being indecisive, confused egos caught in a tug-of-war between the natural and the supernatural!

JOY DOES NOT DEPEND ON CIRCUMSTANCES

Some years ago I was honored to share a meal with Richard Wurmbrand, a former prisoner of the Communists. He had endured severe torture for his faith. I asked if he ever felt as if he were losing his mind. He said he did, but gave those feelings to Christ so that he didn't have to worry anymore. When he suffered heartache for his family, he gave those emotions to Christ as well and he was set free. When he gave his body to Christ, he no longer needed to worry about his health. Armed with complete death to his flesh, the Communists no longer had the power to hurt him.

"The guard came for me one day and said, 'You must realize that I can break your arms, your legs, anything I want.'" Richard told me. "I answered, 'If you break my arm, I will say, God loves you and if you break my leg I will say, I love you too.' With that, the guard began to cry and I was able to lead him to Christ that day."

When we're grafted into Jesus, what shall we fear?

Perhaps this is why Jesus' most frequent admonition to rejoice was:

> *Blessed [happy] are ye, when men shall hate you, and when they shall separate you from their company, and shall reproach you, and cast out your name as evil, for the Son of man's sake. Rejoice [have joy] ye in that day, and leap for joy: for, behold, your reward is great in heaven: for in the like manner did their fathers unto the prophets,* (Luke 6:22-23 [inserts added].)

This was the joy Paul and Silas experienced while in prison in Philippi. They rejoiced in the Lord while bearing stripes on their backs and stocks on their feet in the pit of an ancient Roman jail. (See Acts 16:22-26.) How many of us can say our situations have ever been lower than that? Then what right do we have to be so glum unless we just are not abiding in the plan of God for our lives?

Peter talked of the joy set before us, even in the face of persecution or whatever circumstances might bring:

> So be truly glad! There is wonderful joy ahead, even though it is necessary for you to endure many trials for a while.
>
> These trials are only to test your faith, to show that it is strong and pure. It is being tested as fire tests and purifies gold—and your faith is far more precious to God than mere gold. So if your faith remains strong after being tried by fiery trials, it will bring you much praise and glory and honor on the day when Jesus Christ is revealed to the whole world.
>
> You love him even though you have never seen him. Though you do not see him, you trust him; and even now you are happy with a glorious, inexpressible joy. Your reward for trusting him will be the salvation of your souls, (1 Peter 1:6-9 NLT.)

Persecution will come in this world by one means or another. We know this because even those of us not actively telling others about Jesus experience hardships and trials. Why not instead take such things head-on and experience Jesus' joy through them! Accept God's Word, walk in it, and obey His voice. He will never leave us or forsake us! (See Hebrews 13:5.) After all, what can separate us from His love? (See Romans 8:35.) We as Christians have no reason to be so despondent and filled with worry, *for the joy of our Lord Jesus is our strength!*

> *Always be full of joy in the Lord. I say it again—rejoice! Let everyone see that you are considerate in all you do. Remember, the Lord is coming soon.*
>
> *Don't worry about anything; instead, pray about everything. Tell God what you need, and thank him for all he has done. If you do this, you will experience God's peace, which is far more wonderful than the human mind can understand. His peace will guard your hearts and minds as you live in Christ Jesus,* (Philippians 4:4-7 NLT.)

➤ ◄

CHAPTER NINE

Free from Evil

. . . . thou shouldest keep them from evil.

JOHN 17:15

THE WORLD SEEMS MORE FILLED with evil today
than ever before. Here, in the twenty-first century, we are not
marked by the futuristic Utopia envisioned when my ministry
began in the early seventies, just a few years after astronauts first
landed on the moon. At that time we looked ahead to the new mil-
lennium with starry-eyed wonder at what technology and science
would accomplish. Yet now we live in a time dominated by more
fear, stress, and anxiety than ever before. We seem to be bearing
the fruit of a society that planted self-sufficiency and pride deeply
in our minds as we bought the biggest lie the devil has ever told: We
can go it alone without God.

If we think humanity has truly progressed throughout our history, then we need to take a careful look at the fruit of the last century. In a time when we thought the world was growing increasingly
open-minded and accepting of other beliefs and cultures, we saw
more Christians killed for their faith than in the previous 1,900 years

combined. In fact, in the last one hundred years nearly 65% of all the martyrs that have died since Jesus were murdered.[9]

In the wake of this Age of Understanding, the twenty-first century began with fear that the very technology in which we had placed our hopes would backfire on us. Remember the Y2K scare? The terrorist attack of September 11, 2001 exposed our vulnerability to those with hatred in their hearts. As if this were not enough, our economy and stock market are still reeling because people lied to us again and again about the value of their companies in order to push up the price of stocks—and personal portfolios—while those same actions drove companies to bankruptcy.

Twenty-four hour news channels fill us in on every detail of such crises while circulating the news of wars and rumors of war which Jesus prophesied would come in the final age. Cinema and television are no longer satisfied with "good guys always win" stories—now the heroes of some of the most popular series and films are mobsters, homosexuals, witches, warlocks, thieves, and serial killers. Even the good guys have serious character flaws and dark sides. Moral and ethical issues are clouded by in-depth news reports and talk shows. "What is right?" is a question eliciting more differing opinions than ever before. There have also been more cults and new religions birthed in the last century than in all of history.

How are we who are devoted to Jesus supposed to live and raise our children in a world that seems so bound for hell?

"LORD, KEEP US FROM EVIL"

In John 17:15, Jesus prayed that we should be kept from evil, but with evil seemingly so solidly entrenched around us, what are we to do? Do we just shut ourselves off from the world, turn off the TV and radio, and live as if we were in a monastery? If we are going to separate ourselves from evil, we must dig it up by its roots and cast it out of our lives.

The problem is the real root of evil does not come from outside us, but from within. Before we can deal with society's evils, we must deal with our own.

Evil doesn't begin with adultery, murder, bank robbery, fraud, or genocide; it starts with lives that are empty of God. It starts with boredom, with thinking that you deserve more out of life, and that no one is going to help you get it besides yourself. It breeds where people are determined they want a certain thing and the only way they are going to get it is by pursuing their own desires. They don't know God; they think God is not really interested in them anyway, so why should they be interested in Him? They think they are better off without God's guidance or help. Evil grows as they succumb more and more to selfish, fleshly desires, and then redefine good to fit their own concepts.

Jesus described how evil can come into our lives and grow to take over, blinding us to the truth:

> *Your eye is a lamp for your body. A pure eye lets sun-*
> *shine into your soul. But an evil eye shuts out the light*
> *and plunges you into darkness. If the light you think you*
> *have is really darkness, how deep that darkness will be!*
> (Matthew 6:22-23 NLT.)

What we set our eyes upon determines our focus in life. If we have a pure focus on the truth (the King James Version says "single" here, perhaps contrasting with the "double mindedness" expressed in James 1:6-8), then we will have the light of God in our lives. Rejection of God's truth is fertile soil for evil.

If we focus on half-truths and accept them as whole truths, how great is the darkness that grows within our hearts! Why would we accept half-truths? Because they justify our own concepts more than the Word of God does. They let us live as we want, validating our lifestyles and our lack of real intimacy with God. By accepting half-truths, change is not necessary as we embrace a definition of good defined by the Self on the throne of our lives. We refuse to measure ourselves against the example of Jesus and do not allow Him to order our steps.

If we look at these scriptures in context with what Jesus is saying in this passage, we can see even more about the source of evil:

> Don't store up treasures here on earth, where they can be eaten by moths and get rusty, and where thieves break in and steal. Store your treasures in heaven, where they will never become moth-eaten or rusty and where they will be safe from thieves. Wherever your treasure is, there your heart and thoughts will also be.
>
> Your eye is a lamp for your body. A pure eye lets sunshine into your soul. But an evil eye shuts out the light and plunges you into darkness. If the light you think you have is really darkness, how deep that darkness will be!
>
> No one can serve two masters. For you will hate one and love the other, or be devoted to one and despise the other. You cannot serve both God and money. . . .
>
> He will give you all you need from day to day if you live for him and make the Kingdom of God your primary concern, (Matthew 6:19-24, 33 NLT.)

Here, one might think that Jesus was giving a discourse on God's provision and how we should not love money—and then up pops this little rabbit trail about evil. He then returns to His discourse on finances. But was Jesus changing the subject after all? Throughout this entire passage He is teaching about how God provides for His children.

Remember how I said that evil comes from wanting something you feel life is cheating you out of, and then deciding the only way you can get what you want is to look out for your own interests? Well, this is what Jesus is talking about in this passage: When you want something, how are you planning to get it? Are you going to turn to the world's system for accumulating wealth, popularity, job security, material goods, or whatever it is you are seeking? You think if you have those things you will be happy—have joy—and so you focus on acquiring the things upon which you have set your heart. Within that focus you will eventually be willing to cut corners to get your desires.

For non- Christians this may seem obvious; but I am not talking about those outside the Church. I am talking to those that *call* Jesus "Lord." We attend church regularly, call ourselves Christians, and think we belong to Christ, but our eye (focus) is elsewhere. We may give allegiance to God with our mouths, but in our hearts we are not seeking after God and His kingdom. We are seeking worldly wealth! We really don't believe that following God will get us everything that will make us happy, so we fellowship with other so-called Believers who feel the same way. We compare ourselves to each other, vainly thinking that we are at least better or smarter than most of the people who sit next to us in the pews. Why? Because we have memorized more scripture, spend more time in prayer, lead a Bible study, or some other religious work. We may pray in tongues, cast out demons, or lead others to the Lord on a regular basis. However, if we treasure the things of this world more than the things of God, and then create doctrines to justify those desires, we leave an unsanctified Self on the throne of our lives—and how great becomes the darkness in our souls! We call Jesus "Lord, Lord," but when God calls us to do something to help manifest His kingdom on the earth, we don't hear that call because we are so wrapped up in our own *selves!*

> *Not all people who sound religious are really godly. They may refer to me as "Lord," but they still won't enter the Kingdom of Heaven. The decisive issue is whether they obey my Father in heaven. On judgment day many will tell me, "Lord, Lord, we prophesied in your name and cast out demons in your name and performed many miracles in your name." But I will reply, "I never knew you. Go away; the things you did were unauthorized,"* (Matthew 7:21-23 NLT.)

The *Harper's Bible Dictionary* definition of evil:

> All forms of evil are regarded as ultimately occasioned by *the disobedience and rebellion of the human race with regard to God and God's will.* Evil occurs where and when God's will is hindered by human sin.[10] [Italics added.]

We may be building churches and ministries and kingdoms in His name, but do these things come out of time spent getting to know Jesus, discerning His plans, and then living them? Or have we set our eyes on the good things that can go with such organizations—wealth, reputation, respect, and more—and have in truth gone about using God's name to build kingdoms for ourselves? Are we truly acting in obedience to the Jesus we know through prayer and His Word, or are we simply seeking self-justification by walking religiously before other people? Are we defining our self worth by the standards of His Word or by the accepted practices of our culture and local churches? Is our Christianity based on Jesus or on a conservative American-Christian mindset that makes us think we know better than everyone else? How do I know people like this exist in the body of Christ? Because I have been there!

On one visit to the White House in the 1980s, President Reagan invited me to step into the Oval Office. There he showed me the Bible used for the swearing-in ceremony at his Inauguration. It was open to II Chronicles 7:14. In the margin was a note that read, "Son, this scripture is for the healing of the nations." A plaque on his desk read, "A man can become too great in his own eyes to be used by God." Boy, did I feel important!

But the President didn't stop there. He allowed me to walk with him as he stepped into the Rose Garden. Cameras began to flash and a crowd of reporters waiting behind a roped off area began to shout at him. I felt drunk on my own importance. I had been invited many times to the White House, and realized I was one of about one hundred ministers in the nation to have this privilege.

The President was asking me questions. I was advising him. I thought, "It is so great to have the President of the United States as a friend." With that thought filling my head, he turned to me, shook my hand and said, "Good to see you again, Bob."

What a blow! What was I doing there? At the time it mattered more to me that the President knew my name than that Jesus did! Boy, did I have my wires crossed! My own selfish desire to be famous was leading me into the evil of hypocrisy.

THE ROOT OF ALL EVIL

Paul warned Timothy about the source of all evil :

> *The love of money is the root of all evil: which while some coveted after, they have erred from the faith, and pierced themselves through with many sorrows,* (I Timothy 6:10.)

Vine's tells us that the Greek term for "love of money" is *philarguria* (literally the love of silver) which means "covetous, avaricious."[11] It means simply "selfishness"—(self-on-the-throne-ishness)--which is the root of *all* evil. The *New Bible Dictionary* has a similar definition for *evil*:

> The Hebrew word comes from a root meaning "to spoil", "to break in pieces": being broken and so made worthless. It is essentially what is unpleasant, disagreeable, offensive. The word binds together the evil deed and its consequences. In the New Testament, *kakos* and *ponēros* mean respectively the quality of evil in its essential character, and its hurtful effects or influence. It is used in both physical and moral senses. While these aspects are different, there is frequently a close relationship between them. Much physical evil is due to moral evil: suffering and sin are not necessarily connected in individual cases, but *human selfishness and sin explain much of the world's ills.* [12] [italics added]

I Timothy 6:10 also tells us that those who fall into this trap "erred" in their faith. The footnote in my Bible tells me that *erred* also means "been deceived." Those who walk in selfishness deceive themselves into believing that their ways are right! Their eyes are darkened, and they see everything through a lying filter of self-justification.

> *There is a way which seemeth right unto a man, but*
> *the end thereof are the ways of death,* (Proverbs 14:12.)

Look at how *The Message Bible* paraphrases what Paul says only a few verses earlier:

> *If you have leaders . . . who refuse the solid words of*
> *our Master Jesus and this godly instruction, tag them*
> *for what they are: ignorant windbags who infect the air*
> *with germs of envy, controversy, bad-mouthing, suspi-*
> *cious rumors. Eventually there's an epidemic of back-*
> *stabbing, and truth is but a distant memory. They think*
> *religion is a way to make a fast buck.*
> *A devout life does bring wealth, but it's the rich sim-*
> *plicity of being yourself before God.* (1 Timothy 6:3-6,
> THE MESSAGE.)

The only solution is to get with Jesus and let Him heal our blindness!

> *Search me, O God, and know my heart: try me, and*
> *know my thoughts: And see if there be any wicked*
> *way in me, and lead me in the way everlasting,* (Psalm
> 139:23-24.)

➤ ◄

CHAPTER TEN

Are We Living a Life of Deception?

So, because you are lukewarm, and neither cold nor hot, I will spew you out of my mouth.

REVELATION 3:16, RSV

MOST OF US WILL NEVER reach the level of *evil* where we commit some felony or crime—and in this we think we are alright—yet instead we sink down into a soothing state of being lukewarm that is neither a force for heaven nor a threat to hell. We grow more and more tolerant and complacent, satisfied to live being entertained rather than fulfilled. We watch evil flourish on the news—thinking unconsciously, "Well, at least I'm not that bad"—then turn to a sporting event or a sitcom to numb the spirit within us urging us to pray and seek God's plan for our world. The Bible calls it "searing our consciences:"

> *But the Spirit explicitly says that in later times some will fall away from the faith, paying attention to*

deceitful spirits and doctrines of demons, by means of the hypocrisy of liars seared in their own conscience as with a branding iron, (I Timothy 4:1-2, NASB .)

We become complacent, content to live in our religiosity, to know all of the Christian catchphrases and correct answers, which we can rattle off at the drop of a hat. But we don't really know God or His purpose for our lives. We are in reality building our own kingdoms rather than manifesting His. Just like the religious leaders of Jesus' time on earth, we are so content to live in a reality void of God's grace and miracle-working, life-changing power, that if anyone crosses our path preaching the true Gospel, we would rather call him a heretic and false prophet than to align with the truth.

It might seem logical to interpret the line in the Lord's Prayer, "deliver us from evil" as a request to keep anything bad from happening to us, but we forget that it is preceded by the line "lead us not into temptation." (See Matthew 6:13.) Evil is not on the earth so much to hurt others—which is the world's perspective of evil. It says, "Hey, if I am not hurting anyone else, what's the problem?" The real purpose of evil is to separate us from God. Satan's true intent is to keep us from knowing God, being one with Jesus, and living a life of His present-day ministry through the power of the Holy Spirit. The Devil would rather have an ineffective, hypocritical Christian walking the earth than he would have a serial killer plaguing a community, because the hypocritical Christian is actually more efficient in driving people away from God and towards hell.

LUKEWARM CHRISTIANS HAVE CHANGED OUR NATION

We have lost our confidence to stand up for Jesus, because what is in the world around us seems more real than Jesus does to us. We don't *know* Him anymore! We are numb to the reality of God because we spend all our time focused on things of the world. What the experts say seems more real and relevant than what the Bible says. It is time to renew our minds to what the Bible says and let God show us its relevance!

The dictionary definition of *hypocrisy* is "a feigning to be what one is not or to believe what one does not."[13] But I also like to look at it this way, breaking it down into its parts: hypo means "under" (as in *hypodermic needle*—a needle that goes "under the skin"), and -crisy comes from the same word as "critic," meaning that we are "judging or evaluating." In the same way that "under construction" means something that is not finished, but is still being built. To me, "hypocrisy" means that our beliefs are still under evaluation—we are still thinking about it and have not yet decided what we really believe.

Well, wake up! It is time to get off the fence and decide! If the world system is truth, than follow it, but if God is truth, then follow Him!

If we don't have the time to spend with Jesus and allow Him to fully develop within us the conviction of His truth and His kingdom, we have no right to call Him "Lord" nor any claim to His salvation!

It is our complacency and lack of biblical conviction of truth that is letting our world go to hell! Recent studies indicate that America has moved from the fifth to the third-largest mission field in the world. We have the resources, but we're losing ground. Literally ninety percent of all offerings are spent here and we have fifty-seven million professing Christians who could easily evangelize the entire country. Yet we continue to rise steadily on the list of the most un-churched, un-evangelized people on earth.

Today when we see churches hold revivals, we mistakenly

think we're seeing America revived. But we have to acknowledge that many of us are busy managing our programs and projects, and looking back wistfully at what God has done, content to glory over how Christ's power was manifest in a bygone era instead of permitting Christ to accomplish His work in our time.

The world has, in many ways, taken over the Church instead of the Church taking over the world. Until Self is dethroned and Christ is enthroned in our hearts, the Church—made up of God's people—will continue taking two steps backward for every one step forward. We watch the same entertainment, wear the same clothes, laugh at many of the same jokes, and share the same appetites for fashion, food, and fun as the world. The world has infected, seduced, polluted, and brainwashed us with its entertainment, styles, and lusts. Christian children dress like gang members and foul-mouthed singers. Christian women wear styles inspired by the homosexual fashion world. We never even consider what inspires trends in clothing or entertainment.

How can a Christian teach Sunday school in the morning then go to an R-rated movie that afternoon with graphic violence, nudity, the name of Christ profaned, and filthy language while sitting there placidly eating popcorn with their spouse and children? How can we sing in the choir, greet the visitors, then go home that night to channel surf, watching the most despicable perversions and porn channels, then click off the TV, read our Bible for ten minutes, say a prayer, and never feel convicted? Then we wonder why we're having problems in our lives, our homes, and with our children. It's because Self is on the throne. When we surrender to the flesh, we live in a state of neutrality and appeasement instead of righteousness and holiness.

We may boast that God is moving in our churches. Well, He's

moving all right—moving right out the door of many churches! The name of some churches can just as easily be replaced with "Ichabod," meaning "The glory has departed..." (See I Samuel 4:21.)

In William J. Bennett's book, *The Death of Outrage*, the author scolded Americans for allowing their president at the time, William "Bill" Clinton, to defile the office of the presidency by using it as a gimmick to attract young girls. Instead of rising in outrage against the blatant immorality of social and political leaders, some Christians defend the guilty, while many remain silent. The Senate didn't have the conviction to remove Clinton from office because many of them were absorbed in the same sin! Some wondered, "What's the big deal?" Others were apathetic, because it didn't really affect them personally. We don't seem to fight until something infringes on our own individual rights or those of a loved one. Thus morality isn't the issue; personal comfort is. Why get too worked up about something if it doesn't directly affect us in some way?

But we cannot expect the nation to be more moral than we are. I am here to tell you, *as goes the Church, so goes the nation.* There's been little outrage over tens of millions of abortions, over the profusion of Internet pornography, or over a divorce rate which affects more than half the population—including those in the Church. Statistics indicate that more couples are living together without benefit of marriage than at any other time. There is little outrage over the massive number of teenage pregnancies and suicides in the Church as well as outside it. We've grown accustomed to teen alcohol and drug abuse in our midst—or else we simply turn a blind eye to it, hoping it will go away because we are too busy being entertained to really get involved.

We have no conviction to do right and stand up for God's kingdom because we haven't been with Jesus!

Where's the outrage that more Christians are persecuted worldwide today than at any other time in history? Where's the outrage over multiplied millions dying of AIDS? Where is a Christian's outrage over fatherless children? Over twenty-seven million American children will go to sleep tonight without a father in their home. It is said that ninety-two percent of the young people in the city of New York have never even darkened the door of a church. America leads the world in sexually active teenagers per capita and in abortions.

We show little outrage as states and denominations seek to approve homosexual marriages, and lobby to lower the age of sexual consent—in essence legalizing child molestation. Little indignation is expressed over hard-core pornography, which represents a larger consumer market than Hollywood moviemaking. There is little outrage over crime—even though approximately every twenty-two seconds a major crime occurs in the U.S., and every thirty-four minutes that crime is a murder. Some one hundred thousand students carry guns into classrooms on any given day and at least one in five American children will end up in jail. One million teenagers in America are alcoholics. America leads the industrial world in murder, rape and incarceration. Where is our outrage?

Television shows such as "Who Wants to Be a Millionaire?" became number one in America because instant gratification appeals to our greed. Our attitude as a nation seems to be "Gimme, gimme, my name is Jimmy." Reality shows receive high ratings because they can get women into skimpy clothes, promote nudity, or put people in dangerous, disgusting, or suggestive situations for our entertainment. Television producers have learned to appeal to the lusts of our flesh to get a larger audience—and people are flocking to it! Satan is taking over our airwaves with little more than a peep from the Church. Why? Because as many of us rush home to watch these shows as people in the world do!

This is the spiritual poverty that Mother Teresa spoke to me about so many years ago. As the most powerful nation on earth we have used our position to become comfortable at the expense of a lost and dying world. The Church was to be the light of the world, yet it is obvious that our Christian light no longer dispels the darkness. If this is true, then how great is our own darkness? No wonder it is said that eighty percent of our young people leave the Church when they leave home. They saw that it didn't work for their parents, so why would it work for them?

IT IS TIME TO BE JESUS-JUSTIFIED INSTEAD OF SELF-JUSTIFIED

Unfortunately, it is difficult to fault the media for providing us with the form of entertainment that *we* want, nor can we fault immoral politicians that *we* elect! Though many may not agree with this, morality cannot be legislated. This type of regulation leads to more work for our police forces and legal system. All we can expect is more of the same in this world until we who are in Jesus so influence those around us that they turn off the filth and seek more of God for themselves!

And the only way that will ever come to pass is if we put God's ways and His Word above our own.

If evil comes from selfishness, then it is time to replace that selfishness with Christlikeness. Are we willing to love others with the love of Jesus? Are we willing to bless those that curse us, placing the demand on God to justify us rather than trying to justify ourselves? The only way God can ever keep us from evil is if we walk closely with Him in every area of our lives.

As the former prisoner, Richard Wurmbrand, once said, "As [my persecutors] the Communist atheists allowed no place for Jesus in their hearts, I decided I would leave not the smallest place for Satan in mine." If we are ever to be a threat to evil, then we must have the same conviction!

➤ ◄

CHAPTER ELEVEN

The Truth Shall Set You Free

Sanctify them through thy truth: thy word is truth.

JOHN 17:17

THE YOUNG PROSTITUTE—caught in the very act, they had said—must have looked into the eyes of Jesus that day. She was bewildered as He told her simply, "Neither do I condemn you. Go and sin no more." (John 8:11 paraphrased.)

I have always imagined that she stood there for a moment, still shuddering, holding her torn dress to cover herself, unsure of what to do. She probably looked questioningly at Jesus, then stole a glance at her former accusers, none of whom would now meet her eye, though just moments before they had been ready to assume the role of judge, jury, and executioner.

After a quick glance at them, not wanting to allow time to recover their self-righteous indignation, she must have stolen away as quickly as possible. She had been delivered from a tortuous death by a man brave enough to confront others with the reality of their own sins.

Because of their shame, it is likely no one glanced up to watch her go. I imagine instead they might have scuttled away, avoiding the gaze of the Teacher who had somehow known their most hidden sins. They wanted nothing more than to escape His attention. Yet despite their obvious attitude of menace, Jesus wasn't through revealing to them that the darkness in their own hearts was as black, if not blacker, than that of the prostitute:

> *"I am the world's Light. No one who follows me stumbles around in the darkness. I provide plenty of light to live in."*
>
> *The Pharisees objected, "All we have is your word on this. We need more than this to go on."*
>
> *Jesus replied, "You're right that you only have my word. But you can depend on it being true. I know where I've come from and where I go next. You don't know where I'm from or where I'm headed. You decide according to what you can see and touch. I don't make judgments like that. But even if I did, my judgment would be true because I wouldn't make it out of the narrowness of my experience but in the largeness of the One who sent me, the Father. That fulfills the conditions set down in God's Law: that you can count on the testimony of two witnesses. And that is what you have: You have my word and you have the word of the Father who sent me."*
>
> *They said, "Where is this so-called Father of yours?"*
>
> *Jesus said, "You're looking right at me and you don't see me. How do you expect to see the Father? If you knew me, you would at the same time know the Father."* . . .
>
> *"You're tied down to the mundane; I'm in touch with*

what is beyond your horizons. You live in terms of what you see and touch. I'm living on other terms. I told you that you were missing God in all this. You're at a dead end. If you won't believe I am who I say I am, you're at the dead end of sins. You're missing God in your lives. . . .

"When you raise up the Son of Man, then you will know who I am—that I'm not making this up, but speaking only what the Father taught me. The One who sent me stays with me. He doesn't abandon me. He sees how much joy I take in pleasing him."

When he put it in these terms, many people decided to believe.

Then Jesus turned to the Jews who had claimed to believe in him. "If you stick with this, living out what I tell you, you are my disciples for sure. Then you will experience for yourselves the truth, and the truth will free you," (John 8:12-19, 23-24, 28-32 THE MESSAGE.)

Unable to reach beyond themselves, many never received this truth Jesus so freely offered. They remained trapped in their habits and customs. The teachings of Jesus were outside the litany of answers they had memorized so eagerly at Pharisee school, thinking that always having the correct answer was their ticket to salvation. In fact, they were more bewildered than ever, not because Jesus gave different answers, but that He was asking different questions.

Jesus was presenting what seemed to them to be something new, although it was buried in every chapter of the holy writings. He wanted them to understand that it is not what you *do* as much as it is *who* you know and obey. They wanted to justify themselves by their opinions and actions, keeping the outward commandments to be seen by others, but ignoring the inward issue of repentance and truly following God. They were ready to judge and condemn others for falling short of *their* standards so that all would see their uncompromising dedication to their principles. Yet when the very God whom they said they obeyed walked right into their midst, their self-justifications blinded them. They didn't even recognize Him. They didn't want to know God, but to control, dictate to, and be worshipped by men. Entrapped by sin, they claimed to be free. Yet here was Jesus kneeling before them, presenting the truth with such clarity and sincerity that it became a stumbling block—a crushing stone—upon which they would either build their salvation or beneath which they would be smashed by their own self-righteousness. Meeting the Truth in person left them no other options. (See I Peter 2:6-8.)

As we sit in the pews of our churches today, are we more like those who accepted Jesus and saw what was truly in their hearts? Or are we like the Pharisees who clung to their own traditions, opinions, and half-truths rather than changing ingrained, self-righteous concepts? Are we just as wrapped up in our own beliefs, culture, and desires as they were? Do we justify ourselves by learning all of the correct responses, but miss the real answer? Are we satisfied with how we look to others while Jesus stands nearby grieving at our ignorance of Him?

It is time we come to really know the Truth and let that Truth set us free.

THE TRUTH *WILL* SET YOU FREE

Jesus' fifth prayer was "that they also might be sanctified through the truth," (John 17:19.) The sanctification Jesus speaks of here is the process of being "set apart for God...to make a person or thing the opposite of *koinos*, 'common.'"[14] According to Peter, we are called to be a "peculiar [special or uncommon] people, that ye should show forth the praises of Him who hath called you out of darkness into His marvelous light," (I Peter 2:9, insert added.) Jesus called us the salt of the earth, the light of the world, and a city set on a hill that cannot be hidden. (See Matthew 5:13-16.) That we are Christians should be obvious to others because we speak and act differently. We carry God's light within us. When we enter a room there should be a different atmosphere because the Holy Spirit indwells us.

In one incident, another evangelical leader and I were invited to meet with the President. We flew together to Washington, and checked in at the Hilton Hotel. As my colleague stepped through the doorway, a precious woman who was vacuuming the lobby looked at him and instantly began to weep. She fell to her knees as probably no less than twenty people watched, raised her hands and cried, "God forgive me, I'm a fornicator."

God's presence changes things, so if He is truly in us, then His life-changing power should shine through us. Yet, instead, we are often indistinguishable from the rest of the world. Some might call themselves undercover Christians, but the truth is we're not under-cover; we're unchanged!

Nothing can blind us to that more than ego or self-deception. Sometimes it appears that those who seem to be doing the most for God are the most deceived. In the past three decades, scandals have rocked the Church on an international scale with every vice from greed to adultery to child molestation. Then, as if that were not enough, on the other side have been those of us who stand in judgment over these people, erring on the side of stiff religiosity and driving more away from God because of our unforgiveness and self-righteous demeanor. Believe me, I know what I am talking about here; I have experienced this fleshly pride first-hand.

During the scandal surrounding the demise of the PTL television network in the mid-eighties, I was invited on television news programs—Crossfire, CNN, Nightline, and so forth—to debate the various attorneys involved. Charles Gibson on "Good Morning, America" continued one such show through two extra segments because we were having such an insightful discussion. I thought I was doing a service to the Body of Christ. But instead I was engaging in what Evangelist Doug Stringer called the "Spiritual Immune Deficiency Disease"—*cells eating other cells within the Body.*

Consider all the energy I've wasted over the years seeking the approval of others, becoming intoxicated by someone else's power, working as an unofficial arbitrator in big-name church cases, engaging in media fist-fights all over the nation. I thought I had arrived and was finally really doing something to help Jesus. But Jesus doesn't need such help—He needs my humble obedience. I wasn't carrying out His ministry on the earth—I was blindly exalting Self! I was seeking validation and justification for my flesh. I was allowing it to fight other flesh—and all under the Christian banner!

Like those drunk with wine, those of us drunk with flesh are unreasonable and bleary-eyed. We do not see things clearly or truthfully; we see things as we want to see them, through the haze of self-centeredness. We can go on like this our entire lives, unless we are arrested for a DUI—being Deceived under the Influence of Self. As Christians, we have a choice: We can surrender to God and permit Him to sober us up, or we can choose to cling to the deception that has so entranced us. If we cling to such pretext then we become a poster child for the Devil—Christians trying to live out Christianity by the power of the flesh rather than the power of the Spirit.

As I was collecting my thoughts for this book, I met a businessman who people said was the godliest man in town. He was small and wiry, in his mid-forties with slightly graying temples. He wore a tailored suit that matched his refined manners. We had a long drive together from one part of the city to another, so I spent the time telling him and three other ministers in the van about some of the things I wanted in this book.

After a few minutes I noticed that the businessman had become completely silent, his face turning ashen. Finally he exploded, "God help me! I'm all messed up!" He motioned for the driver to pull off the freeway with tears streaming down his face.

"That's me!" he cried as he paced beside the van. "That's me. I can't live the Christian life. I've tried to do everything right, but I can't."

That was a Holy Spirit intervention! Through the power of the Holy Spirit present with us in that car, our friend came to a point of clearly seeing the truth. Cut to the heart, he accepted it, confessed his sin, and chose to walk more closely with Jesus than ever before! The truth can have that kind of effect on people—suddenly seeing the truth clearly set him free of his own hypocrisy!

ARE WE BLINDED TO THE TRUTH?

When Jesus stood before Pontius Pilate to be tried, they had the following conversation:

> *Pilate said to Him, "So You are a king?"*
> *Jesus answered, "You say correctly that I am a king. For this I have been born, and for this I have come into the world, to testify to the truth. Everyone who is of the truth hears My voice."*
> *Pilate said to Him, "What is truth?"* (John 18:37-38 NASB.)

With Truth standing before him to be judged, Pilate asked the question that has spawned all human philosophy, theology, and, unfortunately, religion, "Pilate saith unto him, What is truth?" (See John 18:37-38.) These are the things people have invented as a way to try to reach God, having rejected the work of Jesus Christ on the Cross.

Staring into the very face of Truth, Pilate rejected Him, desiring rather to hold on to his own opinions and political correctness rather than risk embracing the Truth. He cared more for the sensibilities of the Roman pagans and the Jewish priests. He was too absorbed in protecting his own self-interests and position—too trapped by his own self-conceit. To accept the Truth would set him free. Thus the imprisoned and enslaved always condemn the free, because the truth they offer is more than the self-absorbed and self-deceived are able to bear.

Jesus experienced this with Jewish leaders as well as with Pilate. Those who struggle for a real relationship with God always depend upon the religious leaders of the day, which is one reason the Body of Christ has become so divided. We have forgotten how to be hungry for truth and have grown satisfied with manmade doctrines rather than sinking to our knees and seeking God for the whole truth. It is time we become so hungry for the truth—the whole truth and nothing but the truth—that we let nothing else satisfy us or get in the way of manifesting His truth upon the earth.

Perhaps we have become like Pilate: We need to answer the same question he asked Jesus and be very clear about the response. It is easy to say that the best definition of truth is that Jesus is Truth personified. (See John 14:6, 1:14, 17; Romans 15:8; and Ephesians 4:21.) Only by truly knowing Him can we really know the truth. Through Him are all things revealed:

I am the light of the world: he that followeth me shall not walk in darkness, but shall have the light of life, (John 8:12.)

The nature of light is that in it we clearly see every nuance and detail. Jewelers use a magnifying glass and a bright light to examine diamonds for even the tiniest flaw or imperfection. So will the light of Jesus work in our lives to reveal things that are unseen in the darkness or half-light. If we have His Light, it will reveal the truth of what is in our hearts so that we can prune the dead branches and fruitless activities and grow to become more and more like Jesus everyday. This is why people rarely harvest in the dark—it is hard to tell the wheat from the tares as Jesus told his disciples in a parable:

The kingdom of heaven is like a man who sowed good seed in his field. But while everyone was sleeping, his enemy came and sowed weeds among the wheat, and went away. When the wheat sprouted and formed heads, then the weeds also appeared. The owner's servants came to him and said, 'Sir, didn't you sow good seed in your field? Where then did the weeds come from?' 'An enemy did this,' he replied. The servants asked him, 'Do you want us to go and pull them up?' 'No,' he answered, 'because while you are pulling the weeds, you may uproot the wheat with them. Let both grow together until the harvest. At that time I will tell the harvesters: First collect the weeds and tie them in bundles to be burned; then gather the wheat and bring it into my barn,' (Matthew 13:24-30, NIV.)

When Self is on the throne our vision is dimmed by half-truths we accept to justify our ambiguous lives. Even a half-truth is a whole lie. We live in the darkness and shadow of Self not seeing things clearly. It is like walking into a room to find your car keys, seeing them on the counter in the shadows, and upon picking them up only to discover that you have instead picked up a tarantula! We can be so mistaken in the way we see things that we are deceived into accepting untrue doctrines and beliefs. However, since in the half-light they justify our desires and appear to be the very thing we desire, we embrace them wholeheartedly. Thus instead of the truth of God, we build our self-image on the foundation of culture, habit, and environment. We have little time or inclination to examine a thing too closely to determine its true nature. Thus, finding ourselves comfortable, we complacently settle for just a little knowledge of God rather than being hungry for much more of Him.

Look again at what Jesus said to these Pharisees:

> *You decide according to what you can see and touch. I don't make judgments like that. But even if I did, my judgment would be true because I wouldn't make it out of the narrowness of my experience but in the largeness of the One who sent me, the Father . . . .*
>
> *You're tied down to the mundane; I'm in touch with what is beyond your horizons. You live in terms of what you see and touch,* (John 8:15-16, 23 THE MESSAGE.)

Those religious leaders were deceived because they accepted the natural world as the sole evidence for the truth. Knowing nothing of the spiritual, they simply excluded it. Not knowing they had an open door to God if they would only seek Him with all of their hearts, they never knocked on it for entry. They were quite happy to accept their own little world of friends and philosophy as all that was needed for life and godliness. In their deficiency they claimed to be whole, shutting God out from their midst.

Jesus however said that even though He lived in the same physical world they did, experiencing the same things and reading the same scriptures, His judgment could be counted on as righteous. Why? Because He didn't judge "out of the narrowness of My experience but in the largeness of the One who sent Me, the Father," (John 8:12, The Message.) By becoming one with His father, Jesus understood the true from the false. He was not limited by the *natural* because He had experienced the *supernatural* by spending time with His Father. His only limitation would have been the lack of a relationship with the Father.

> This is perhaps also why Jesus said,
>
> *If any man come to me, and hate not his father, and mother, and wife, and children, and brethren, and sisters, yea, and his own life also, he cannot be my disciple,* (Luke 14:26.)

Anyone who is not willing to make Jesus the preeminent source for truth rather than, "Well, my family believes . . ." or "My pastor says . . ." or "I read in a book by such and such minister that . . ." is really not His disciple. Anyone who lives mainly by what another says is not following Jesus, but someone else.

I am not saying that ministers and books cannot help us come to know God in a more intimate way, but have you truly examined the gems of wisdom you have received from them in the light of Christ and His Word? Or are you simply following something that sounds good to you because it scratches an itch for something new? Look at what Paul said about such itching ears:

> *For the time will come when men will not put up with sound doctrine. Instead, to suit their own desires, they will gather around them a great number of teachers to say what their itching ears want to hear. They will turn their ears away from the truth and turn aside to myths,* (II Timothy 4:3-4 NIV.)

➤➤ ◂◂

CHAPTER TWELVE

The Leader's New Anointing

*And ye shall know the truth,
and the truth shall make you free.*

JOHN 8:32

DO YOU REMEMBER the children's story of "The Emperor's New Clothes"? How a con man came to a small kingdom with a vain ruler, posed as a tailor, and made the king a new suit of clothing out of "fabric so fine that only the most refined can see it?" Because all those in the palace wanted to get ahead in the royal administration, they didn't have the courage to say that they couldn't see the fabric or the suit of clothing. They couldn't admit that they weren't refined. It would be the end of their careers. They would no longer be accepted and respected by their peers. So the con-man tailor spun a suit out of nothing and pretended to sew these pieces together to make the king's garment. Then, on the great day of presentation, the king decided he would see who in his kingdom was refined and who was not. So he called for a parade. He put on his "new suit" and walked—naked as the day he was born, I believe the expression is—out into the village. For more than three quarters of the route, no one said a word other than "oohs" and "ahs" of admiration—they were all too ashamed to admit that the emperor was naked. What would everyone else have thought? This went on, of course, until a small boy who knew nothing of what was refined or why he should lie, pointed his finger and shouted, "The emperor has no clothes!" At this point the entire crowd saw through the ruse and began to laugh uproariously. The emperor responded by grabbing a coat from someone to cover himself, and stole back to the palace in shame.

The truth had set them all free!

Paul warned Timothy there would be a time in the Church "when people will not listen to the true teaching but will find many more teachers who please them by saying the things they want to hear. They will stop listening to the truth and will begin to follow false stories," (II Timothy 4:3-4, NCV.) Like the emperor in the story, some ministers often parade new messages before a congregation—claiming a special anointing or a unique touch of God upon their lives—hoping for big offerings or greater acclaim. They teach messages that comfort the fleshly desires of people or make promises of what God will do if they only give offerings large enough to really show their faith in God. Pastors parade new programs, ushering in seeker-sensitive messages that neither offend nor convict. Such things as respect, compassion, and physical well-being should not be ignored. However, a person who does not know Christ should never be made to feel at home in the church. It is the convicting power of the Holy Spirit that draws a person to Christ, not the music or the message.

Whole denominations have proclaimed the standards of the Bible passé and have welcomed perversion into their midst as alternative lifestyles or other paths to God.

It is time someone stood up and said, "The preacher has no anointing!"

In the later years of Israel's history, the Ark of the Covenant was completely empty. It had originally held the tablets on which were written the Ten Commandments—a symbol of God's holy Law—and the staff of Aaron that had budded as a symbol of God's supernatural power. This emptiness must have grieved the Spirit of God, but the people continued conducting their rituals.

In a like manner, have millions of Christians in America today accepted outer religious appearances in place of the real Spirit of God? Like Israel in a bygone era, we hear things such as "I went to the Ark Sunday." "I gave toward the Ark." "I sang in the choir at the Ark." Are we affirmed by the Ark—the outward appearance of being religious—or forgotten what was supposed to be inside the Ark—the law and power of God?

Israel's reverence was never to be for the Ark, but for what it represented—God's presence. Although Believers claim to have received more revelations of God today than in any previous generation, we can't seem to move past Self into the supernatural power available to us. The Ark held the Word of God and was symbolic of the power of God, but if we are more enamored of outward appearances rather than Jesus dwelling within us, then we are white sepulchers—beautiful and clean on the outside, but filled with deadness within. (See Matthew 23:27.)

> But realize this, that in the last days difficult times
> will come. For men will be lovers of self, lovers of money,
> boastful, arrogant, revilers, disobedient to parents,
> ungrateful, unholy, unloving, irreconcilable, mali-
> cious gossips, without self-control, brutal, haters of

good, treacherous, reckless, conceited, lovers of pleasure rather than lovers of God, holding to a form of godliness, although they have denied its power; Avoid such men as these, (II Timothy 3:1-5 NASB.)

Far too many Christians today are more interested in using Christianity to get what they want out of life rather than allowing Christ to use them to reach a lost and dying world. We want a religion that justifies us and makes us feel better about ourselves, rather than religion that transforms us into the image of Christ.

And those of us who feel that we are the least susceptible to this are perhaps more vulnerable to its deception. At one time the Charismatic church was the fastest growing denomination in the United States; thousands joined in just one decade. They joined this movement believing that all Jesus did in His ministry was for them, and yet within that group were tens of thousands *experiencing nothing of this power in their own lives.* They shouted the loudest, but did they really do anything else to manifest God's kingdom on the earth?

JUST THE PLAIN AND SIMPLE TRUTH

We—the entire Body of Christ (especially in the United States)— have become too easily lulled into fleshly complacency—the cause of our spiritual poverty. We are caught up in our accomplishments rather than Christ's ministry. We no longer love truth, only what the truth can *do for us.* Thus when truth is inconvenient, we ignore it. Or, as has become the norm today in business, politics, and the Church, we spin the facts the way we want them. Sometimes there is not much difference between putting things in their best light and lying. Those who spin the facts are more interested in appearance than substance.

Another level of truth is what is actual and factual, plain and simple. We know how difficult being truly objective is in a situation, but those who have been with Jesus should be the most objective people on earth. They should be able to be completely honest with themselves, knowing their own faults and shortcomings, and speaking to their own hurt if necessary, for the sake of the truth. (See Psalm 15:4.)

Perhaps education has been a good example of this. In the past, teachers have been instructed to be very critical of students as if the harder they were on them, the better. Yet we found this to be damaging to the self-confidence of students. It follows suit that poor self-confidence leads to poor marks. More recently, teachers are trained to be very positive, no matter what the students does, to build their confidence, hoping that eventually this will lead to overall improvement. What in fact has happened is that we have a generation of students who now confidently make mistakes, and when confronted often scoff at the rebuke.

This positive spin is seen repeatedly in the business world. Large corporations, so intent on presenting a positive outlook to shareholders, have gone from putting things in the best light to actually misreporting the numbers and lying about the value of their companies. We have seen the same thing in the Church: Ministers refusing to admit their human frailties until a point of total meltdown has been reached. They are then forced to step down from the pulpit because of sin or burnout.

The Bible, however, doesn't tell us that being constantly critical or always looking at things in a positive light is the answer to growing up in Christ. Ephesians instead advises us:

> *That we henceforth be no more children, tossed to and*
> *fro, and carried about with every wind of doctrine, by the*
> *sleight of men, and cunning craftiness, whereby they lie*

in wait to deceive; But speaking the truth in love, may grow up into him in all things, which is the head, even Christ, (Ephesians 4:14-15.)

It is the *truth* that will set us free in every situation, and not the truth as seen through rose-colored glasses, which often distorts the facts. I believe this is one of the reasons Jesus told us to judge not. (See Matthew 7:1.) When we add to the truth, we put ourselves in a position to be judged just as executives from big business are judged in our courts for accounting misrepresentations. We need to get back to the basic wisdom of Joe Friday on "Dragnet" so many years ago, "Just the facts, ma'am."

Let your statement be, "Yes, yes" or "No, no"; anything beyond these is of evil, (Matthew 5:37 NASB.)

Let your yea be yea; and your nay, nay; lest ye fall into condemnation, (James 5:12.)

IT IS TIME TO REPROGRAM

Of the thousands of decisions we make daily, how many do we consciously consider before acting upon them? Chances are, very few. What *is* directing our lives then? Habit—patterns accepted over time are repeated and justified. They become so ingrained that we don't even think before we act. We are trained by what we accept as true, and that training becomes an instinctive reaction that directs our every step. Then if those things that we have accepted are half-truths, we stumble around in the dark rather than scrutinizing them through the light of God's Word!

Such deception rarely goes from point A to point Z in an

afternoon. Seldom does a person start in the ministry one day and the next is in bed with someone else's spouse! Hardly ever does a hard-working employee begin a new job with the long-range goal of embezzling from the company. Who would even consider marrying someone who they knew would someday commit murder? Though we could never imagine such things in the beginning; these things happen daily in our society—and in the Church! Pastors run off with their secretaries; ushers pocket money from the collection plates; loving spouses murder their mates for one reason or another. "If then the light within you is darkness, how great is that darkness!" (Matthew 6:23 NIV.)

The acceptance of a half-truth is like smoking a cigarette. Little by little as we inhale, the nicotine darkens our lungs. After years and years of this, they turn black and can't be penetrated even by x-rays. Smoking saps our breath and ages us prematurely. Illness creeps in until we are no longer of use to our families and those who depend on us. Sin, like cancer, grows until it takes over our entire life. Acceptance of these lies sears our conscience to the point that the voice of God no longer can penetrate the heart—the black lump within.

However, sin is not the real problem. Just as cancer is the result of taking in smoke from cigarettes, sin is the result of ingesting the half-truths that justify Self on the throne. It is flesh carried away by lusts that brings about sin. (See James 1:15.) Sin is the fruit, flesh is the root. When we repent of sin, we're dealing with the fruit, which is very important. But cutting out the root, which is Self on the throne, is even more important.

Most evangelists, myself included, have preached against the *fruit* of the flesh—drinking, drugs, lying, and lust. Great numbers of people go to the altar, pull the fruit off their flesh, and two weeks later return to the same altar having committed the same sins. Repentance must deal with the *root*. If we deal only with pruning the branches, allowing the tree to live, we only guarantee a bumper crop of sinful fruit for the next revival!

John the Baptist said One was coming to lay the axe to the root of the tree. (See Matthew 3:10.) We don't just want to prune a little cruelty, unforgiveness, or lying. No matter what we do to the fruit of sin, if the axe is never laid to the root, we miss the reason Jesus came. We must sever the flesh root and become grafted into the True Vine—Christ. *Truth is the axe which will separate the root from the rotten fruit!*

It is the person of the Holy Spirit who gives us the power to see our flesh from an eternal standpoint —from the perspective of absolute Truth. Flesh-fed Christians have boasted, "There is therefore no condemnation to them which are in Christ Jesus," but never realize that the rest of that Scripture is, "who walk not after the flesh but after the Spirit." (Romans 8:1.)

We must become absorbed in the truth of God's Word—renewing our minds. As Paul wrote in Romans 12:2:

> *And do not be conformed to this world, but be transformed by the renewing of your mind, that you may prove what is that good and acceptable and perfect will of God.*

Habit can be reprogrammed to work in our favor.

> *You have been believers so long now that you ought to be teaching others. Instead, you need someone to teach you again the basic things about God's word. You are*

like babies who need milk and cannot eat solid food. For someone who lives on milk is still an infant and doesn't know how to do what is right. Solid food is for those who are mature, who through training have the skill to recognize the difference between right and wrong, (Hebrew 5:12-14 NLT.)

In other words, if we feed on God's Word and grow up in Him, there will come a time that even our physical senses will know the difference between good and evil and act accordingly without a second thought—this is flesh dominated by the Spirit! This is truly life with Jesus completely on the throne of our lives! It is time that we grow up enough to accept the meat of the Word and make a lasting difference for His kingdom on the earth!

DO YOU LOVE TRUTH MORE THAN YOUR OWN REPUTATION?

In speaking of the end times and those that would follow false prophets, the Bible tells us:

They perish because they refused to love the truth and so be saved, (II Thessalonians 2:10 NIV.)
If we say we have fellowship with Him and yet walk in darkness, we lie and do not practice the truth, (I John 1:6 NASB.)

Do we truly love truth? Those who risk being one with Jesus will find that His light will reveal much in their life that is harmful and should be abandoned; yet the good fruit that comes from His Spirit will thrive in this light. Jesus on the throne will shine this light into every nook and cranny and expose everything that needs to be changed or eradicated. This is exactly what needs to happen if we are to be sanctified—set apart—for His use.

This is not something that will happen overnight, neither will we arrive at a place where one day we can sit down and say *"Now I am holy."* It is an every-day pruning process we must go through every day, and that always hurts. But the opportunities to have Jesus truly work through us to touch other lives makes it all worthwhile. I can imagine nothing greater than meeting Jesus on that day when I too have finished my race (see II Timothy 4:7-8) and hear Him say, "Well done, thou good and faithful servant: thou hast been faithful over a few things, I will make thee ruler over many things: enter thou into the joy of thy lord," (Matthew 25:21.)

It is time to draw close to God, basking in His Light and allowing His Truth to set us free from anything that might keep us from accomplishing His plan for our life on earth.

➤➤ ◄◄

CHAPTER THIRTEEN

Savor the Glory

. . . that they may behold my glory, which thou hast given me.

JOHN 17:24

ON THE DAY OF PENTECOST, people from many nations were saved and the foundation of the Church was established in the known world through the testimony of those in Jerusalem. In less than three hundred years, the Roman Empire, which had ruthlessly persecuted Christians for much of its history, was thought of as a Christian empire. In the first centuries, God touched various men who sought Him—Polycarp in the church at Smyrna, an African named Tertullian, an Egyptian named Antony, and others. God's power was also seen dramatically, if only occasionally, in the fourth and fifth centuries as an Italian, Jerome, translated the Bible into Latin, and the Libyan Augustine, wrote the classic, *Confessions.*

Throughout the Dark Ages, Christian slaves who were shipped to other parts of the world spread the Word of God and revival came to their captors. A young slave named Patrick escaped, but then returned to his former masters in Ireland with the power of God upon his life. The nation was transformed by the Gospel of Jesus

Christ. In the fourteenth and fifteenth centuries, God's power again became more evident. In England, the outpouring of the Holy Spirit influenced a young man, John Wycliffe, to translate the Bible from Latin to English. A hundred years later, William Tyndale introduced a new English Translation from the original Greek. Around this time, a German, Martin Luther, saw the corruption in the Catholic Church and sparked an entirely different kind of revival when nailing his famous Ninety-Five Theses to a chapel door in Wittenberg.

The nation of India saw flames of revival in the sixteenth century. In one instance, a minister named Francesco ordered bystanders to open the day-old grave of a dead man. The holy man fell to his knees, prayed, and commanded the dead man to rise. The man arose in perfect health—and the whole village turned to God.

Even school children have been visited by God. History records three hundred children prophesying in Cevennes, France, at the end of the seventeenth century. The children's revival lasted over a decade until it was forcibly subdued by the French army in 1711.

Moravian exiles saw revival in Germany in 1727 when a regular meeting was disrupted and all fifty in attendance fell under the power of God. They established a twenty-four hour prayer chain, which remained unbroken for one hundred years. Their missionaries greatly influenced two ordinary brothers named John and Charles Wesley.

In 1739, God touched the Wesley brothers and revival spread in Europe. George Whitfield, who fell under the power of God at their meetings, preached the first open-air sermon in England in four hundred years. People cried out under the power of God in his services—something that troubled the twenty-four-year-old evangelist. But a countess wrote to him, "Don't be wiser than God. Let them cry out. It will do a great deal more good than your preaching."

In the meantime, at least 50,000 people, one-fifth the entire population, were converted in New England between 1737 and 1741, as God used a young evangelist named Jonathan Edwards. This revival touched a young student at Yale College, David Brainerd, who left school to minister to the tribes of the greatly feared Native Americans. God's power that enveloped his meetings was described as "a mighty rushing wind."

The "Great American Awakening" started unexpectedly on a Sunday in 1857 at an Ontario, Canada, Methodist Church when— without any call for salvation—twenty-one people repented and were saved. The church had no full-time minister, but the lay pastor, recognizing God's divine power, held daily services. The move led to thousands of conversions.

That same year in New York City, Jeremiah Lamphier, an ordinary businessman led by God, organized a noon prayer meeting near Wall Street. On the first day, four businessmen joined him. That grew to twenty; soon the number doubled. Then the worst financial panic in history struck. Banks closed. Men lost jobs. Families went hungry. Within six months, ten thousand businessmen gathered for prayer. Twenty other groups evolved. At a time when the population of America was only twenty-six million, an estimated one million people were converted in just two years. It literally shook the nation.

Neutralized and unbelieving generations have waited for the coming of Christ, not realizing He was there with them all the time. John G. Lake was a normal layman who felt the call of God and pioneered more than five hundred churches in Africa even though the bubonic plague was decimating the inhabitants of the land. His health astonished doctors who couldn't understand why he did not contract the disease. At one point, he challenged the doctors to take some foam from the plague, check it under a microscope, and then put it on his hand. When they scraped it off his hand and again inspected it under the microscope, they were amazed to see that all signs of the disease had vanished. As in the case of the Apostle Paul who went about his business unharmed after having shaken off a venomous viper, the bystanders were amazed. (See Acts 28:3-5.)

Such men and women do not try to fulfill their own plans or visions, but operate in the ministry of Jesus Christ! The spirit of life in Christ Jesus makes them free from the laws of sin and death. (See Romans 8:2.)

In 1904 a woman in India formed prayer groups of girls, numbering five hundred strong. They saw prayer answered in July, 1905, when revival broke out in many Indian cities, including Bombay (now Mumbai.) Two decades later in China, the Norwegian missionary Marie Monsen's prayer groups met twice daily for seven years until revival came. At roughly the same time in Rwanda and Burundi, East Africa, several discouraged missionaries called for a week of prayer and humility before God. Within a decade, fifty thousand people were converted.

After the Second World War, in the Outer Hebrides Islands, off the coast of Scotland, two sisters in their eighties, one blind and the other arthritic, began to seek God for revival. Twice daily, they prayed for every person by name and for the inhabitants of each cottage in their village. Unbeknownst to them, seven young men were also praying in a nearby barn three nights each week. One night after repenting before God, the young men fell to the floor by the power of God.

The next day, one of the women related to her pastor a vision she'd had the night before of the island's deserted churches packed with people. He then invited Duncan Campbell, a young minister from Scotland, to speak. Duncan's first night in revival was uneventful, but after dismissal on the second night, the entire congregation halted outside the church, unable to leave the grounds because of the power of God. When they went back inside the church, the holy presence of God filled the stone building. Within months revival encompassed the island.

THE GLORY OF GOD BRINGS REVIVAL

I deviate from the traditional meaning for revival, and define it as "a supernatural visitation within the Church and also within the world." It is a supernatural new awakening.

Revival is within us, waiting to be stirred up as on the day of Pentecost. Revival is not merely a service, big crowds, enthusiasm, repentance, or great worship. If we define revival as simply a state of being revived, quickened, or filled with God's presence, and not split hairs over the word, we can say that Christ lived on earth in perpetual revival. He was filled with the presence of the Father. That's why, when He saw a widow's grief at the loss of her only son, He reached out and touched the dead boy, who instantly sprang to life. (See Luke 7:11-16.) Now, that's revival!

Revival is what happens to Believers when they are fed up with being fed up. They become hungry and thirsty for God, and won't settle for anything else. It happens to people whose prayers are like that of Moses:

> *If thy presence go not with me, carry us not up hence.*
> *For wherein shall it be known here that I and thy people*
> *have found grace in thy sight? is it not in that thou goest*
> *with us? so shall we be separated, I and thy people, from*
> *all the people that are upon the face of the earth. . . . I*
> *beseech thee, show me thy glory, (Exodus 33:15-16, 18.)*

Moses asked for God's continual presence and His glory follows when He is welcomed.

LORD, SHOW US YOUR GLORY

The Westminster Confession of Faith states that the chief purpose of man is to glorify God and enjoy Him forever. Jesus' sixth prayer in John 17 was "that they may behold my glory, which thou hast given me," (John 17:24.) God's glory follows His presence and touches lives. This is true revival. Throughout history His glory has come in bursts as individuals have yearned for God's presence. As we have just seen, amazing revivals would break out in areas as a result, but each time they fizzled out. Is this what God has planned for us? Or have we—as did the children of Israel (see Psalm 78:41)—limited what God really desires to do?

The destiny of nations, as well as our individual calling, is linked inexorably to God's purpose. "For whom he foreknew he also predestined to be conformed to the image of His Son," (Romans 8:29.) Our destiny is to be like Jesus. Yet even the most sincere attempts to concentrate on a single set of religious goals through willpower and self-discipline leaves the life untouched. We become only partially transformed, suffering moral inequality, in which one part of our nature becomes overfed, while the other is starved. This is trying to live out our Christianity in the flesh through willpower. God's hope for our future is quite different.

And we, who with unveiled faces all reflect the Lord's glory, are being transformed into his likeness with ever-increasing glory, which comes from the Lord, who is the Spirit, (II Corinthians 3:18 NIV.)

The Greek word for "glory" is *Doxa* from which we get the word Doxology. As Believers, we must show the glory of the Lord as if we were mirrors reflecting His face. Our children are most often a reflection of us. We can imitate books we've read, family and friends with whom we have come in contact, for they become part of who we are. We absorb into our innermost being what we reflect and those we habitually admire. As I have said before, we are a product of the truth we embrace.

We cannot change ourselves just as we cannot pull ourselves up by our own bootstraps. Every man's character changes and develops as it is influenced by outside forces. Often, we have failed to place ourselves in the path of such forces. Through self-dependence, struggles, efforts, and agony, we try to control circumstances, but only Christ can change us. The Word of God speaks of clay and the potter. (See Isaiah 64:8.) Clay cannot mold itself; it needs the Master Potter to transform us into His design.

Jesus said:

> *I have set before thee an open door that no man can shut, for thou has little strength and has kept My Word and has not denied My Name,* (Revelation 3:8.)

Jesus showed us that one way to open the door is to have little confidence in our own strength. We live in a generation in which we love to boast about how much power *we* have. Christ always works through those who recognize how much power *He* has.

The fishermen who became disciples were raw, unspiritual, uninspired men. But the Bible says these ordinary, unschooled men astonished everyone because they had been with Jesus. (See Acts 4:13.) Being with Jesus changes us from "glory to glory." (See II

Corinthians 3:18.) Paul was immersed in Christ. When we intently dwell in the Highest, we reflect the Him.

> *For I am confident of this very thing, that He who has*
> *begun a good work in you will perfect it unto the day of*
> *Jesus Christ,* (Philippians 1:6.)

When we try to repair our damaged sense of identity, or heal the wounds of our own heart, we get ahead of the first order of business and risk placing ourselves in the center of our universe. Self-interest becomes the dominant concern. Flesh always resists even the slightest demand of the Spirit. Christ will be reflected in us with all His glory when we have dealt with our stubborn commitment to self-centeredness.

The pathway to revival is clearly marked. It always begins by admitting we are not yet where we need to be with God, and then builds the desire within us to conform more closely to the image to which God has called us. It is one thing to be willing to pray, but another to become a living prayer. It is one thing to make a sacrifice, another to become a living sacrifice. We too often believe we can make a small sacrifice for Jesus—thinking that is enough—rather than obeying and being a holy sacrifice by placing control of our lives on the altar of God.

> *Therefore I urge you, brethren, by the mercies of God,*
> *to present your bodies a living and holy sacrifice, accept-*
> *able to God, which is your spiritual service of worship,*
> (Romans 12:1 NASB.)

Christians today tend to use the phrase, "God is moving," and yet you won't read of the Apostle Paul telling people the Holy Spirit was moving; He just moved. I'm afraid that sometimes when people emphasize the Holy Spirit moving, He is moving right out of the building, because the attention is not on Him and His work, it is on the works of the flesh. We may have so little Holy Spirit power that we spend an enormous amount of time witnessing to each other rather than allowing the Holy Spirit to bear witness of Himself.

Pastor David Yongii Cho once said to another pastor who has since passed away, "You're a Holy Ghost atomic bomb." The pastor became very excited.

"Really?" he said. "Has God showed you anything else about my ministry?"

"Yes," Dr. Cho said, "He showed me you're trying to blow up a piggy bank!"

Here we are as professing Christians, stewards of the greatest power on earth, great enough to create an entire universe from nothing, yet what are we doing with it? Are we just using it to get into other people's piggy banks? Why seek pennies when you can have eternal change? *God's power isn't to be used to take, but to give.*

GOD HAS BIGGER PLANS

The late Pastor David Wilkerson, a friend for many years, once said to me as he commented on a great revival, "This is not that."[15] He was not diminishing the power of the revival; he was saying, "Before there can be a great awakening that shakes America, there had to be a rude awakening." That's what's coming next. The shaking of cities and entire nations!

God has decreed an end-time manifestation of His power and glory that will shake the world and take us beyond Pentecost, beyond mere revivals. He will take us beyond ourselves.

We want what we've been promised—the present-day ministry of Jesus operating unhindered within us.

It's time we each see such a move of God in our lives! Christians today comprise thirty-three percent of the total world population, over two billion strong, yet only a fraction has experienced the present-day ministry of Christ. Think what can be accomplished when we all do!

When great saints pray, a flame of the Spirit is stirred up from within. Instead of praying, "God, send revival," they all discover the same thing: The Person of Jesus Christ revealed by the Holy Spirit *is* revival. We need to stand up at His command and declare His presence. Declare God's Glory! It's all about Jesus! When we ultimately become acquainted with Jesus, we are drawn into the presence of the Father which leads us to His glory!

I was at a church outside New Orleans many years ago when, before I preached, Jesus softly instructed, "Stand up and declare a spirit of salvation." I thought, *How odd*. But I obeyed.

When you say what Jesus says, you will see what Jesus sees and you will do what Jesus does.

When I spoke Christ's words, instantly the power of God fell on that congregation. The large chandelier began to shake; then the building shook. I was told later that the pastor's wife called the police to ask if there had been an earthquake. There had not been, but sixty-two people who did not know Christ, rushed from their seats to the altar for salvation.

The visitation of God's glory is a heaven-sent revival, the Holy Spirit power within us manifesting the present-day ministry of Jesus Christ. All we need are hearts hungry enough to believe His Word and act upon it in His wisdom.

The Church in the Book of Acts caused demons to tremble.

Christians preached the Word with fire and glory; there was nothing they wouldn't do for God. There were no territorial rights, no spirit of competition, no power plays, no arrogance and no big egos.

The great teacher E. M. Bounds said, "Programs, techniques, campaigns are utterly useless unless people are under the control of the Holy Spirit. Men are God's methods. While men look for better methods, God looks for better men." You and I can be among those for whom God is looking!

DON'T TELL ME HOW REVIVAL STARTED, TELL ME WHY IT STOPPED

Perhaps the greatest question for us today is not how revival is born, but what kills it? It is hard to believe that God would reach out to His people, touch them briefly, then intentionally retreat to leave them stranded. Before Jesus returns, the Gospel will almost certainly have to spread around the world in at least one last revival. Will we be part of that, or a hindrance to it?

To the Apostle Paul, his fleshly self was not a mere setback, not a drama or a hurdle to be overcome; it was a fatal wound, a deadly disease.

I used to think I should be horrified by my flesh, that I should control it, squelch its evil, and discipline myself unto righteousness. But Paul went far beyond that, saying he was never surprised at what his flesh was capable of, because in his flesh dwelled "no good thing." (See Romans 7:18.) We need not expect ourselves to be better than we are. We must allow the transcendent life of Christ to transport us beyond our flesh. What we cannot control, Christ can transcend if we allow Him entry.

When we're squeezed, what's inside comes out. Because darkness is increasing as we move toward the end of the Age, more pressure will come to bear upon every Believer. The flesh has to be dealt with so only the Spirit of God emerges.

> *The people who do know their God will be strong and do exploits,* (Daniel 11:32.)

This prophecy will be fulfilled through those of us willing to pay the price.

We cannot live until we first die—to sin, to Self. This is the greatest paradox in history. The Israelites were given only one use for animal flesh—to burn it. (See Leviticus 6:8-13.) Daily, priests robed in ceremonial attire carried the flesh outside the camp and carefully arranged the burnt offering on the altar so that no flesh escaped the flames. They constantly added more wood to the fire. Revival today is the fire of God, sent so we can die to our flesh and become alive to His Spirit.

Why hasn't the message of repentance changed the world? It's been preached to men and women by some of the greatest orators and ministers, with sweeping revivals following. But the spirit behind each movement died because people repented for sinful deeds—the fruit of our flesh, not the root of it—then left thinking they were holy. The battle is not sin against righteousness, but flesh against Spirit.

The Word of God calls us "children of wrath" (See Ephesians 2:3) when we fulfill the desires of the flesh. We wrestle against our own flesh, and never enter the real fight, which is against principalities, powers, rulers of darkness, and spiritual wickedness in high places. (See Ephesians 6:12.) No wonder the Apostle Paul said he wanted to be delivered from this "body of death."

As punishment for murder in Israel and the Roman Empire during Paul's time, the murderer would be chained to the dead body of their victim. The murderer would live with that decaying corpse until the dead body killed the living body. The Apostle Paul understood that his dead and decaying flesh would kill his spirit in much the same way.

FLESH HAS SQUELCHED REVIVAL!

The flesh loses its hold as we live in Christ. This is the difference between religion and life.

> *Walk in the Spirit and ye shall not fulfill the lust of the flesh,* (Galatians 5:16.)

What kills revivals? Religion does. Religious flesh that is manipulative, competitive, angry, jealous, and covetous. Flesh creates divisions within the Church—as many, if not more, than are outside the Church.

Once we've truly known Christ, human religion will never again satisfy. We'll cry out, "There has to be more!"

As did the priests of old, we must daily ensure every scrap of the flesh—its entire works, its lusts, and its ego—is burned. Then the fire of revival can blaze. We have never yet put enough flesh on the fire to keep revival flames burning!

Religious flesh stands at the door of the Holy of Holies with hands folded, smugly believing we have been with Jesus in our quiet times, but blocking the entrance to the glory of God.

English evangelist Leonard Ravenhill stated, "A man that has been with Jesus will never fear Man." That most live to please others before pleasing God testifies against them, and yet we wonder why demons do not tremble and our prayers are not answered. As long as we make people our primary preoccupation, we will be disqualified from going beyond hit-and-miss revivals to the greatest awakening the world will ever see.

The world is waiting for God's Spirit to descend upon us like a royal insignia pressed into the wax of a sealed document. (See Ephesians 1:13.)

We can't convince a lost and dying world to embrace the Good News until we deal with the bad news—that we, God's people who have been called by His name, have not humbled ourselves. We have failed to pray. We have not sought His face. We have not repented from our wicked ways. (See II Chronicles 7:14.)

Yet God still has a people determined to be of no personal reputation so that Christ might be all in all, Lord of Lords, and King of Kings. God is cultivating a people who are hungry and thirsty to give up the low life of being people pleasers to attain the life of Christ.

A lost and dying world will cry out for what we have when they see that we have been with Jesus. It will not be because of what we say, but by the glory of God manifested through our private and public lives. The heavens will open when the flesh surrenders to the present-day ministry of Jesus Christ, allowing God to rule and reign. If anything can make us despise our sinful flesh, it is the true revelation of the price Christ paid at the Cross. If the Christian life can be lived in the flesh, then Jesus died in vain.

Being with Jesus is for those who will pursue His presence. And His private presence has always come before His public power. Noted evangelist D. L. Moody said, "Let us remove all hindrances to revival that come from ourselves. Revival must begin with us."

Every time the world has seen a glimpse of Jesus from one of the great revivalists, people have repented. Imagine what would happen if the world could see the life of Jesus in millions of Christians whose fires burn brightly every day. Satan fears that the Body of Christ will learn to love the smell of burning flesh consumed by the fire of the Holy Spirit, because it will release the glory of God like the world has never seen before. It is that glory which will have to come before Jesus can return. God is waiting on us to wait upon Him.

➤➤ ◄◄

CHAPTER FOURTEEN

Are You Perfect?
If Not, Why Not?

. . . that they may be made perfect in one.

JOHN 17:23

IN 1991, I ENDURED over eight hours of surgery on my neck. I was in pain, depressed, broken, and terribly worried that I might never preach again. But as I lay in bed, only a week and a half after surgery, Jesus spoke to my heart to go to the Middle East. Desert Storm had been initiated and Jesus was sending me from a surgical ward to a war zone! One of the places on that trip was Iraq, where I preached in a field to refugees day and night for a week until finally what little strength I did have was gone and my voice was hoarse. I didn't realize that my weakened condition had placed me in a perfect position for answered prayer from God.

The Holy Spirit softly urged me to preach on Jonah and Nineveh as my last sermon. I taught the best I could on how Jonah finally obeyed God. When he went to Nineveh, the King repented and a great revival broke out, but Jonah was disappointed. I was also disappointed because when I challenged the people to come forward and accept Christ, only one old man came. My interpreter asked, "Why aren't you rejoicing?"

"I'm happy for one soul," I said, "but I was hoping for more."

"My dear brother," the interpreter explained, "the one soul who just found Jesus is the current King of Nineveh! He is the Kurdish Sheik of sixteen provinces, the capital of which is on the site of ancient Nineveh. He has accepted Jesus and has invited you to visit Nineveh; he believes if you preach, they will repent."

Despite my inadequacies and flaws, it turned out I was the right person in the perfect place to make known God's kingdom on earth. In my obedience, God replaced my weaknesses with His strength and I was ideal for the job at hand.

THE PERFECT SOLUTION

Jesus' seventh prayer in John 17:23 is "that they may be made perfect in one." Much too often we define perfect as "without flaw or defect; unblemished and pure, lacking nothing." We might say, "I'm not perfect and never will be. Jesus was the only perfect man who ever walked the earth." Or we think of the end product of an assembly line: Each individual item rolling down a conveyer belt looking exactly like the one before it. In these cases, each product's perfection is measured by how closely it fits the original design.

In this sense and using this definition only, it is true that not one of us is perfect. Certainly none are without flaw or defect, lacking nothing, or matching someone's standard of perfection to which we were all originally meant to conform. But the definition of perfect in the Bible is somewhat different. It is important to know the biblical meaning of perfect to fully understand what Jesus was praying for us.

In the Old Testament, the word "perfect" is translated from the Hebrew word *tamiym*, meaning "complete, whole, entire, sound, healthful, wholesome, unimpaired, innocent, having integrity; what is complete or entirely in accord with truth and fact."[16] It is the word used to describe a lamb that would be sacrificed as a sin offering. If a sheep can be considered perfect then why not a person? This perfection is not related to the lack of character faults, but *the fitness of the thing for the task at hand.*

The word perfect in John 17:23 is the Greek word *teleioo*, which means: 1) "to carry through completely, to accomplish, finish, bring to an end. . . . . 2) [to] add what is yet wanting in order to render a thing full. . . . 3) to bring to the end (goal) proposed. 4) to accomplish."[17] A slightly different derivative of this root word is defined as "1) brought to its end, finished; 2) wanting nothing necessary to completeness. . . . 4) full grown, adult, of full age, mature."[18]

Another word translated as perfect in the Scriptures is *katartisis*, which means: "a making fit . . . implying a process leading to consummation."[19] In other words, in the Scriptures, perfect is more a meaning of being "fit for" or accomplishing something, as in the fulfillment of prophecy. This is one aspect of how Jesus was perfect: He was the perfect sacrifice to complete the promise of the law; He is the Alpha and Omega, the beginning and the end. In this sense, we too can be perfect as we conform to God's plan to help manifest God's will for someone.

In this light, it is easy to see that a totally imperfect (modern meaning) vessel or tool can be perfect (biblical meaning) for a given task. A plug with a nick in it may be the perfect fit for a hole that has a rough edge. We would say they fit together *perfectly* even though both parts are imperfect. It may also be that we design something, say a tool, that is unique, a serious deviation from the original design, so that it can accomplish a very special designated task. A tool may be redesigned for a man who has lost a finger so that it will fit perfectly into his hand.

At the age of 31, I faced one of the greatest crises of my life. I had been working eighteen hours a day, seven days a week, striving to be the best I could be. I had no comprehension that I was competing for acceptance among my peers. I was addicted to work in the same way an alcoholic is addicted to alcohol, or a drug addict is addicted to drugs. That addiction began to break my health.

An undiagnosed neurological disease began to manifest itself. It caused all the muscles in my neck to spasm. I began to experience panic attacks, and tachycardia. My heart rate would jump from 80 to 200 beats in a matter of seconds.

In the midst of the darkness, I became depressed, discouraged, and physically drained. I cried out to God from the midst of that cardiology ward, "Lord, I've never wanted to know You in the fellowship of your suffering, but I do now." As I said that the Lord said, "Then you shall know Me in the power of My resurrection. Because you are willing to admit what you are not, I will empower you with what I am. Where those two points meet, destiny will be manifested in your life." Little did I know that several months later, the soft, gentle voice of the Holy Spirit would speak to me to read the following:

> *Remember not the former things, neither consider the things of old, behold I will do a new thing. Now it shall spring forth. Shall ye not know it; I will make a way in the wilderness and rivers in the desert,* (Isaiah 43:18-19.)

Through this Scripture it was as though a drop of water had fallen on my parched spirit. Next the Holy Spirit instructed me to go home, send a fax to Israeli Prime Minister Menachem Begin, and ask if he would meet with me. I argued, "No Lord, there's no way. He doesn't even like me, so why would he want to see me?"

Eventually, I obeyed His voice and sent the fax telling Prime Minister Begin I'd be in a Jerusalem hotel for six days and desired to meet with him. I flew there, checked in, and began to pray.

On the second day, I found myself in the Prime Minister's office. I approached him with "Hello, how are you?" He then talked for almost thirty minutes, which was good because I had nothing to say.

Finally he asked, "Why did you come?"

"I don't know why I came."

"You don't know?" he said with astonishment. "What *do* you know?"

"God sent me," I said.

"God sent you but didn't tell you why?" he asked, becoming amused at the situation.

"No, He didn't tell me why," I said, somewhat embarrassed.

He called for his secretary to come into his office.

"Eight thousand miles, Kadashai, to meet with me, and he says nothing except God sent him. Kadashai, shake his hand. We have finally found an honest man!"

Then he turned to me and said, "When God tells you why, will you come back and tell me?"

After leaving the Prime Minister's office I still didn't know why I'd gone, so I prayed and waited for an answer. Finally Jesus softly spoke one word to me, "Bridge." Once I had that, I called and we met again.

As before, after our greeting, he asked, "Why did you come?"

I only had the one word, so I said, "To build a bridge."

"A bridge? Like the Brooklyn Bridge?" the Prime Minister asked. "What kind of bridge?"

I had no idea what to answer, but as I opened my mouth, out popped, "A bridge of love." Immediately Jesus' soft voice became clear on the inside of me as to what He intended for my life through this meeting.

"A bridge of love," he mused. "For whom?"

"Between Christians in America and Jews in Israel," I answered.

"I like that," Begin said again. "I will help you."

That was the start of more than three decades of a Jesus-blessed ministry to the nation of Israel. It revolutionized my life, and helped develop the bridge Jesus wanted to build.

By my not caring about my reputation, God was able to use me. Somehow I fit into His plan, allowing my imperfections to draw me closer to Him.

DEFINING "PERFECT" GOD'S WAY

The prayer of Jesus was that His Church would be "perfect in one," or you might say "complete in unity." In this sense we see that perfection can never be realized without the entire Body of Christ. As an orchestra cannot fully operate without a violin or percussion section, we in the Body of Christ are imperfect when we are not working together as God designed. Each individual part deals with what it is supposed to do just as the parts of an engine must function correctly and in unison with the others for the engine to provide sufficient power to move the car. Paul wrote:

> He [God] gave some, apostles; and some, prophets; and some, evangelists; and some, pastors and teachers; For the perfecting of the saints, for the work of the ministry, for the edifying of the body of Christ: Till we all come in the unity of the faith, and of the knowledge of the Son of God,

unto a perfect man, unto the measure of the stature of the fullness of Christ: That we henceforth be no more children, tossed to and fro, and carried about with every wind of doctrine, by the sleight of men, and cunning craftiness, whereby they lie in wait to deceive; But speaking the truth in love, may grow up into him in all things, which is the head, even Christ: From whom the whole body fitly joined together and compacted by that which every joint supplieth, according to the effectual working in the measure of every part, maketh increase of the body unto the edifying of itself in love, (Ephesians 4:11-16.)

By finding our unique function and destiny within His Body, we become part of His work—fitting perfectly into His plan for manifesting His kingdom on the earth. It is time we stopped saying, "What do you expect? Nobody's perfect!" and become perfect through the knowledge, presence, and wisdom of God. After all, we are commanded in His Word to be perfect. Would God command us to try to achieve something He knows we could never attain?

The Lord appeared to Abram, and said unto him, I am the Almighty God; walk before me, and be thou perfect, (Genesis 17:1.)

Thou shalt be perfect with the Lord thy God, (Deuteronomy 18:13.)

Let your heart therefore be perfect with the Lord our God, to walk in his statutes, and to keep his commandments, as at this day, (I Kings 8:61.)

Be ye therefore perfect, even as your Father which is in heaven is perfect, (Matthew 5:48.)

If thou wilt enter into life, keep the commandments.
He saith unto him, Which?
Jesus said, Thou shalt do no murder, Thou shalt not commit adultery, Thou shalt not steal, Thou shalt not bear false witness, Honor thy father and thy mother: and, Thou shalt love thy neighbor as thyself.
The young man saith unto him, All these things have I kept from my youth up: what lack I yet?
Jesus said unto him, If thou wilt be perfect, go and sell that thou hast, and give to the poor, and thou shalt have treasure in heaven: and come and follow me, (Matthew 19:17-21.)

The disciple is not above his master: but every one that is perfect shall be as his master, (Luke 6:40.)

Finally, brethren, farewell. Be perfect, be of good comfort, be of one mind, live in peace; and the God of love and peace shall be with you, (II Corinthians 13:11.)

How is it that we have so easily rejected perfection as being unattainable? What have convention and culture robbed from the Church because we think perfection is beyond our grasp? If God has commanded us to be perfect, then did He command us to do something that we can never hope to accomplish? Or is there some misunderstanding of the term that is shutting us off from the enabling power that God is trying to bestow upon us?

➤ ◄

CHAPTER FIFTEEN

Growing in Perfection

*Therefore, leaving the discussion of the elementary
principles of Christ, let us go on to perfection...*

HEBREWS 6:1, NKJV

IF WE ALSO THINK that perfection is one point at which we
arrive, and that once achieved it is all that is necessary, look at what
Paul had to say to the Philippians:

> *Brethren, I count not myself to have apprehended:
> but this one thing I do, forgetting those things which are
> behind, and reaching forth unto those things which are
> before, I press toward the mark for the prize of the high
> calling of God in Christ Jesus. Let us therefore, as many
> as be perfect, be thus minded,* (Philippians 3:13-15.)

Obviously, we need to change our thinking in several areas.

Here is another opportunity for us to change our conventional
thinking and come into agreement with the prayer of Jesus. If we

are commanded to be perfect and Jesus prayed that we would be perfect, then it must follow that *we are able to become perfected.*

The simplest way I can think of to define this perfection to which we are called, in the biblical sense, is being in the right place, at the right time, knowing the will of God, and being ready to perform it.

During our first crusade in India, the Holy Spirit told me we would see the greatest harvest of souls ever. I'd never been to India, and my flesh was saying, "They don't know you, they don't know your reputation, no one will show up." To this Jesus softly replied, "Be grateful, it's a blessing; therefore, the only reputation they will know of is Mine."

The night before the crusade began, I had a vision. I saw the throne room of God and Jesus. Next to them were hundreds of idols. Jesus asked, "Whose idols are these?" I was going to say, "They're the idols of India," but I stopped when I saw the names on them. Jesus had revealed my own idols to me. When I awoke my pillow was a sponge of tears. I fell like a dead man on my hands and knees, and crawled into the next room.

My teenaged daughter, Shira, joined me weeping, and soon the entire crusade team tiptoed into the room and joined us in prayer. All night we travailed, emptying ourselves out before the Lord.

I felt like the most unqualified man in the world to preach the next day. Yet more than 250,000 Moslems and Hindus came to Christ that week! People flew from all over the nation and lined up outside my hotel room door. The line of people wanting prayer stretched all the way down to the street. Even a government leader wanting prayer came with his aide. Jesus had shown up in His glory!

What I thought was imperfect, Jesus called perfect for the job at hand. I just had to change the way I viewed things.

Paul's attitude was that he was already perfect—fit and ready to do the will of God in any place at any time. At the same he was striving for more of God, a more intimate relationship with Jesus, and a greater influence of the Holy Spirit in his life. He was pressing "toward the mark for the prize of the high calling of God in Christ Jesus," (Philippians 3:14.) Today's English Version paraphrases this as "God's call through Christ Jesus to the life above." (See Philippians 3:14 TEV.) The *Message Bible* translation for this passage states:

> *Friends, don't get me wrong: By no means do I count myself an expert in all of this, but I've got my eye on the goal, where God is beckoning us onward—to Jesus. I'm off and running, and I'm not turning back.*
>
> *So let's keep focused on that goal, those of us who want everything God has for us. If any of you have something else in mind, something less than total commitment, God will clear your blurred vision—you'll see it yet! Now that we're on the right track, let's stay on it.*
>
> *Stick with me, friends. Keep track of those you see running this same course, headed for this same goal. There are many out there taking other paths, choosing other goals, and trying to get you to go along with them. I've warned you of them many times; sadly, I'm having to do it again. All they want is easy street. They hate Christ's Cross. But easy street is a dead-end street. Those who live there make their bellies their gods; belches are their praise; all they can think of is their appetites.*
>
> *But there's far more to life for us,* (Philippians 3:13-20 THE MESSAGE.)

Here the line "as many as be perfect" is rendered "those of us who want everything God has for us." Does this sound like those who are committed to manifesting God's kingdom on the earth? Does it sound like you?

ARE YOU READY?

We have already talked a good deal about truly knowing Jesus; becoming one with Him, His purposes, and His present-day ministry, as well as other things we need to do to know His will and obey it, but are we *ready* to perform it? Are we ready to do the greater works Jesus said we Believers would do? What exactly do we need to carry out these good works of God?

One thing the scriptures tell us about this is in Paul's advice to Timothy:

> *Be diligent to present yourself approved to God as a workman who does not need to be ashamed, accurately handling the word of truth. . . .*
>
> *Now in a large house there are not only gold and silver vessels, but also vessels of wood and of earthenware, and some to honor and some to dishonor. Therefore, if anyone cleanses himself from these things, he will be a vessel for honor, sanctified, useful to the Master, prepared for every good work.*
>
> *Now flee from youthful lusts and pursue righteousness, faith, love and peace, with those who call on the Lord from a pure heart. . . .*
>
> *All Scripture is inspired by God and profitable for teaching, for reproof, for correction, for training in righteousness; so that the man of God may be adequate [KJV*

says "perfect"], equipped for every good work, (II Timothy 2:15, 20-22; 3:16-17 NASB [insert added].)

A large part of being ready to do the will of God at all times is
being thoroughly grounded in His Word. No, I'm not talking about
what others have taught you, not what your church says about it, or
what you have read in commentaries or other books (this was, after
all, the error of religious leaders in Jesus' day), but *what the Word
of God says to you plainly and simply.* Yes, it is possible that you may
need to work through some of these things with other Believers and
ministers to separate truth from the errors caused by our own human
thinking and misunderstanding. After all, a large part of reaching
perfection is working in community with other members of the Body
of Christ.

The question is not whether you have yet attained, but rather are
you searching? It is the strangest thing, but truth seems to exist more
in the pursuit of it than in the realization—more in the journey than
the arrival. Somehow the people who think they have reached the
highest truths are often farthest from them, but those who are the
hungriest and most desperate seem the closest. There is something in
our openness to seeking the truth—the whole truth and nothing but
the truth—that allows God to speak to us more clearly; while something in the belief that we have already attained that truth deafens us
to His voice and endeavors to reach us with the revelation we need.
Whether this is because we fall into pride, sear our consciences, or
are simply walking in deception, I don't know. What I do know is
that at the moment I lay aside the shovel and stop digging with all
my might for the gold of God's truth and presence by thinking I have
finally arrived, I am led to a moment of despair. It is then I realize I
was much farther from God than I thought. My personal solution has

been to continue to seek Him with all my heart at all times—thirsty for His presence and hungry to do His will. Anything less is to let Self slip stealthily back on the throne of my life and lead me toward the rocks of yet another shipwreck.

For example, if we accept the idea that we are truly perfect in Christ—as a new revelation and a point of attainment—then we might begin by changing the way we speak. We can then say, "I *am* perfect through what Jesus has done for me on the Cross!" Now, there is nothing really wrong with this. In fact we should change the way we speak, for our mouths speak what overflows from our hearts. (See Luke 6:45 NASB.) If we have this revelation firmly implanted in our hearts, then that is what should come out. You need to look at what the Bible says about perfection if you still find yourself casually saying, "Well, no one's perfect!" Obviously, your mind is telling you that you still do not fully believe the truth of God's Word.

The problem is that it is very easy for us to stop at the point of changing the way we speak without truly letting it alter the way we live. We never seem as interested in living a godly life as we are in looking good before others. It is too easy to get caught up with being certain that we always say the right thing and knowing the right doctrine. This then just becomes another list of manmade rules. It is another way of giving lip service to God while Self sits more and more securely on the throne of our hearts! (See Matthew 15:8.)

This is why Jesus so adamantly warned us not to judge teachers that come to us by the accuracy of their doctrines and what they say, but by the fruit that comes out of their lives and ministries:

> *Beware of false prophets, which come to you in sheep's clothing, but inwardly they are ravening wolves. Ye shall know them by their fruits. Do men gather grapes*

of thorns, or figs of thistles? Even so every good tree bringeth forth good fruit; but a corrupt tree bringeth forth evil fruit. A good tree cannot bring forth evil fruit, neither can a corrupt tree bring forth good fruit. Every tree that bringeth not forth good fruit is hewn down, and cast into the fire. Wherefore by their fruits ye shall know them.

Not every one that saith unto me, Lord, Lord, shall enter into the kingdom of heaven; but he that doeth the will of my Father which is in heaven. Many will say to me in that day, Lord, Lord, have we not prophesied in thy name? and in thy name have cast out devils? and in thy name done many wonderful works? And then will I profess unto them, I never knew you: depart from me, ye that work iniquity. Therefore whosoever heareth these sayings of mine, and doeth them, I will liken him unto a wise man, which built his house upon a rock: And the rain descended, and the floods came, and the winds blew, and beat upon that house; and it fell not: for it was founded upon a rock. And every one that heareth these sayings of mine, and doeth them not, shall be likened unto a foolish man, which built his house upon the sand: And the rain descended, and the floods came, and the winds blew, and beat upon that house; and it fell: and great was the fall of it. (Matthew 7:15-27.)

Do you understand what Jesus is saying here? Someone may be sitting next to you in the pew, saying the same thing, singing the same songs, but with a heart far from God. (Look at the parable of the wheat and the tares—Matthew 13:24-30—for another example of this.) The fruit in their life is the only way you can tell where their heart really is, not by what comes out of their mouth! They may even appear to do the works of God and operate in the gifts of the Holy Spirit, but in truth the way they live in private, away from the crowd, has a great deal more to do with selfishness than godliness. When push comes to shove, their decisions will be based on what is best for them, ignoring the dictates of God's love and His Word, while they speak of faith in biblical phrases in an attempt to justify their actions. More often than not, they have even deceived themselves and only the presence of the Holy Spirit will enlighten them and bring them to the truth. (See John 16:8-11.)

Don't fall into the trap of feeling that you are somehow special once you can say, "I am perfect," while the rest of the Body of Christ is blind to this biblical fact. You were special to God long before you learned this and equally special afterward! Neither should you take it upon yourself to correct the rest of the Body when they say, "Nobody's perfect!" What you should do is keep your mouth closed and learn *to live it!*

Jesus, His Word and His will become a threefold cord that is not easily broken, so is aligning what we say with what we believe and what we do. Our words and beliefs are meaningless without our actions. As James said, "Faith without works is dead." (See James 2:20.) That is why we see the lives and ministries of too many unraveling; they are now tasting the bitter fruit they have sown for so long as they continue to preach and teach one thing while living another. You can say Christ is on the throne of your life, but if you don't obey Him and His Word, then it is Self to which you are in submission, not Jesus.

When you are hidden in Christ, Satan can only see Jesus. It is not *your* righteousness which is revealed, but that of Christ. Our concern is not to be perfect or righteous, but to be *in Christ.*

BE LIKE MICAH

I hope I haven't made this sound complicated, because it really isn't. We just have to be honest and like Micah who said:

> What can we bring to the LORD to make up for what we've done? Should we bow before God with offerings of yearling calves? Should we offer him thousands of rams and tens of thousands of rivers of olive oil? Would that please the LORD? Should we sacrifice our firstborn children to pay for the sins of our souls? Would that make him glad?
>
> No, O people, the LORD has already told you what is good, and this is what he requires: to do what is right, to love mercy, and to walk humbly with your God, (Micah 6:5-8 NLT.)

We are called to do right, love mercy, and walk humbly before God day by day. If we do this, constantly seeking His whole truth to meet our daily needs, ready at all times to obey His voice and His Word, then the rest will take care of itself. And that *rest* is the wildest, most joyful ride you could ever hope to take! It is living the life above on the earth below. Do this, and God inside you will become so real that His presence will change the world around you!

It is time we became answers to the prayers of Jesus! Are you ready to do His will?

➤➤ ◄◄

CHAPTER SIXTEEN

Living Epistles

*. . . that the world may know that thou hast sent me,
and hast loved them, as thou hast loved me.*

JOHN 17:23

*Now they saw the boldness of Peter and John, and perceived
that they were unlearned and ignorant men, they marveled; and
they took knowledge of them, that they had been with Jesus.*

ACTS 4:13

HAVE YOU BEEN with Jesus?

Another great element of becoming perfect—a vessel fit for the Master's use—is *time*. As human beings, we tend to spend our time concerned with what we value most. A person in love spends a great deal of time thinking of his/her significant other. A parent with a demanding job tends to be unavailable at home when their minds are always focused on business. Most of us tend to obsess over the things we think give our lives the greatest meaning and value.

In this way, new Christians often seem obsessed with witnessing and learning everything they can about God because of the profound and redefining impact being born again has had upon their lives. Yet this first love too often turns to complacency as other things in our lives crowd out our time with Jesus (See Revelations 2:4-5; 3:15-22.) Somehow faith turns to mental assent, passion turns to tolerance, and we learn "Christianese" as a way of pleasing people. We have little concern as to what heaven thinks about how we live our daily lives. On the outside we live to get the acceptance of others, whether they believe in God or not, while in our heart, Self and its desires become more and more firmly enthroned.

It is one thing to know something intellectually, but quite another to be able to live it on a daily basis. Just as how knowing the correct golf or tennis swing intellectually rarely means that we play perfectly on the course or court, the only way to make the transfer from brain to performance is to spend time practicing what you know until it becomes second nature. In the military, soldiers practice readiness and learn to perform defense techniques they may never use, or only use once in their entire lives. Paul likened us to such soldiers. (See II Timothy 2:3-4.) We need to put into practice the principles of God's Word to the point that when we hear and obey His voice we are available to be used for His glory.

The book of Hebrews tells us we can get into the milk and meat of the Word to the point that even our physical senses—our subconscious—can tell the difference between good and evil (see Hebrews 5:12-14). We need to walk with Jesus on such a consistent basis that His voice is always clear to us, and we are ever ready to perform His will. When Moses descended from the mountaintop, he had to cover his face because it glowed from God's presence (see Exodus 34:29-35). His presence should dwell within us to the point that the world takes notice. This comes from spending time with Jesus. It was with this thought in mind that Paul called the Believers in Corinth living letters documenting the goodness of God as a spiritual testimony of Jesus:

You are our letter, written in our hearts, known and read by all men; being manifested that you are a letter of Christ, cared for by us, written not with ink but with the Spirit of the living God, not on tablets of stone but on tablets of human hearts, (II Corinthians 3:2-3 NASB.)

Can those around you tell that you have been with Jesus?

BECOMING THE WALKING WILL OF GOD

The eighth prayer of Jesus in John 17 was that people would know God had sent Him and that they would also know we, his followers, are just as loved by God as He was. (See John 17:22-23, 25 and Acts 4:13.) How can the world know how much God loves us unless His love becomes outwardly evident in our lives? When is the last time someone *accused* you of being a Christian?

When Peter entered the courtyard of the palace the night Jesus was being tried, he was accused of having been with Jesus. In response, he denied it. He was accused three times and he denied it three times. He was afraid that having been with Jesus would cost him his life. He couldn't have been more correct. Being with Jesus will cost you everything.

If any of you wants to be my follower ... you must put aside your selfish ambition, shoulder your cross, and follow me. If you try to keep your life for yourself, you will lose it. But if you give up your life for my sake and for the sake of the Good News, you will find true life, (Mark 8:34-35 NLT.)

Today we don't have to deny having been with Jesus. No, it is not that we have a freedom to be Christians that didn't exist in the Roman Empire. It is that no one would ever accuse us of being Christians. No one would even suspect it. When our lives reflect nothing of Jesus in our daily walk, then there is not enough evidence to convict us of having been with Him. When we try to live a Christian life in our own strength and power, we become miserable failures. We play at Christianity on Sunday morning or during midweek service or Bible study, but the rest of the time we are focused on fulfilling our fleshly desires in our own selfish way. The world looks at this and judges our bitter fruit with more honesty than do those to whom we should be most answerable.

In his booklet, *The Mark of a Christian*, based on John 13:35, Francis A. Schaeffer wrote:

> Our love will not be perfect, but it must be substantial enough for the world to be able to observe or it does not fit into the structure of the verses in John 13 and 17. And if the world does not observe this among true Christians, the world has a right to make the...awful judgment which these verses indicate: That we are not Christians...Love...is the mark Christ gave Christians to wear before the world.[20]

We don't hold each other accountable, because we don't want to be held accountable ourselves. Our fellowships and communities of faith are often just social clubs for those desiring to climb the religious ladder, seeking to gain the respect of other people. It has very little to do with what God wants done on the earth. Hypocrisy is one of the greatest tools Satan has for building his kingdom—encounter by encounter, relationship by relationship, soul by soul.

Yet, when only one person dares to spend time with Jesus and begins to live His present-day ministry, it can change an entire generation.

Around the turn of the twentieth century, students at a Bible school in Topeka, Kansas, determined to spend time with Jesus and in His Word, and revival broke out on the campus. After searching the scriptures for what it meant to be filled with the Holy Spirit, they could find nothing to indicate it was not for their day, nor any valid evidence that the gifts of the Spirit were not for all Believers. At this revelation, one of the students stepped forward and asked that hands be laid on her—as was done for Believers in Acts 8:14-17—so she might receive the infilling of the Holy Spirit. When this was done, she was instantly filled and began speaking in tongues just as they did in Samaria roughly nineteen centuries earlier. Soon everyone in the school had received the gift of the Holy Spirit.

Eventually this blessing touched the life of William Seymour, a poor, one-eyed, demoralized African American living before the civil rights movement was even a dream. This touch on his life inspired him to spend time with Jesus. This unknown man started holding meetings in a burned-out mission building on Azusa Street. From this came a revival that has proven to be one of the greatest strategic victories in Christian history. The Gospel was not just heard, but *experienced* through the gifts of the Spirit, as it was embraced by Believers. The Pentecostal Movement that began with those meetings is still a fast-growing part of the Body of Christ.

This movement at the beginning of the twentieth century continues to touch His Church; God is still looking for men and women who will earnestly seek Him. He calls His Church to spend time with Him so that He can touch it afresh in the twenty-first century. He is looking for those willing to be part of the answer to the prayers of Jesus.

This will not happen until we plug ourselves fully into the source of all answered prayer. Time spent at church services, Bible studies, listening to teaching tapes or CDs, watching Christian programming, reading Christian books or whatever we might do to learn about God are good things, but they cannot replace time spent with Jesus. We spend too much time flying by the seat of our pants spiritually, and not enough time on our knees physically. I would even venture to say that if you don't spend time praying every day then you don't believe in God as much as whatever it is that you *do* spend your time doing. An idol can be made of anything if it is given greater attention than that which you give God! It is time to return to our first love and our passion for the presence of God!

In my early years of ministry, I made the circuit of Full Gospel Businessmen's meetings, relating the only part of my testimony I could bear to admit. I was desperately trying to become a superstar as the Jewish boy who was converted. Standing in my pinstriped suit in a hotel ballroom one day, I was praying with people when Jesus softly whispered, "Get out of here!" As usual, I argued because I didn't believe it was proper for the guest minister to run out on the prayer line, but I finally submitted and walked away.

Out on the busy New York street, I felt impressed to walk several blocks and then kneel. It was so embarrassing; I knelt on one knee as if to tie my shoelaces, even though I was wearing loafers without laces. But the person of the Holy Spirit weighed heavily on me. I finally knelt on both knees and began to weep almost uncontrollably. God was breaking that pinstriped show-off who thought he was so important he couldn't leave the prayer line. Jesus breathed, "Son, your obedience in your private life will determine the degree of anointing on your public life."

The crowds had continued to shuffle past me throughout this

episode, but as I arose, one scruffy-looking man carrying two bottles of wine pointed at me and said, "You're weird." It must be of God when weird people call you weird!

Like the little child Jesus called to Him and who came so simply without question or regard to what he had been doing, we must obey His prompting in our private lives before His strength will manifest in our public lives. This can only come from spending time with Him.

Have you been with Jesus?

LIVING *HIS* LIFE

God wants us to live and breathe in Him. The Lord of glory knows why we don't. We read the Bible and pray. We attend church. Whether we know it or not, we practice empty rituals just as the Pharisees and Sadducees did in Jesus' day. We've been bound by the lie that we have to struggle to live the Christian life rather than letting Christ live it through us—that God is not going to use us in a big way as He did the early disciples because that was only for their time—or we are not as holy as they were—or any of the million excuses we use to keep from seeking the perfect will of God.

Wrong! Jesus will be manifested in the lives of hungry saints in order to gather in the final harvest. They will form the army described in the book of Joel, one that will live the end-time ministry of Jesus on this earth. Will you be part of His army?

Why allow the person of the Holy Spirit to pass over us? He can only use those willing to take the next step and die to their flesh. If we are willing, then we can be part of the end-time ministry of Jesus!

Status quo holy-Joe Christianity doesn't work, only Christ-centered Christianity does. We need a vibrant relationship with a living God that will allow His power to change our lives and the lives of those around us. This is Christianity worth living and dying for.

God wants us to do holy works just as Jesus did: Works that reach souls. Why else would Jesus have told us that Believers would do His works?

Shouldn't there be some way—other than Christian T-shirts—that people know we supposedly have been with Jesus? Shouldn't being with Jesus make us different somehow; make us stand out?

God is looking to do great things through us, if we are only willing to be with Him and walk where He directs us. Spending time with Jesus is not something we do once; it is something we live breath by breath.

CARVING OUT QUIET TIME

How does such a vibrant relationship come? Just how does one spend time with Jesus? Is it just a matter of spending hours in prayer? Is it a matter of meditating on every scripture that you read in the Word of God? Is it praising Him at the top of our voice? Or weeping bitter tears of repentance before Him?

All of these may happen in a time of coming before the Lord, but that is not necessarily spending time with Jesus. We can do these in our flesh just as easily as any other religious practice we observe in order to make us feel better about ourselves. However, by truly spending time with Jesus we reach a place of spiritual attentiveness and quiet in order to hear His voice clearly, learn obedience, and allow His Spirit to prune away the dead wood in our lives. Then we can bear the fruit He has designed us to bear. Quietness of spirit comes from being able to focus on God. This often happens after a time of prayer, praise, repentance, and meditation on the Scriptures. It is a place where we have quieted

Self and all the voices of this world to focus solely on seeking His face. As God said through the psalmist:

> *Be still, and know that I am God: I will be exalted among the heathen, I will be exalted in the earth,* (Psalm 46:10.)

The Hebrew word *raphah* is translated here as "still", which means "to sink down, let drop, be disheartened . . . withdraw . . . abandon, relax, refrain, forsake . . . to be quiet."[21] Four of the top translations of the word elsewhere in the *King James Version* are "feeble," "fail," "weaken," and "alone." It seems to have a note of surrender, silence, and abandonment to it.

Being with Jesus is a matter of letting all other things drop, setting all else aside, and focusing only on Him. There is a singularity, a simplicity, and a vulnerability that go with it. It is not something that can be done in five minutes. It may take more than hours at first. To maintain it may demand an occasional quiet weekend. But it is also a place that is easier to attain with practice, though it also gets deeper and deeper the more you practice the presence of Christ. It is being still before God, alone in perfect honesty, seeking Him and His kingdom with all your heart. It is a place of resting and trusting in Him more than anything else, knowing that His ways are above our own, and sitting in His presence as children sitting with their Father. It is a place of comfort and correction, instruction and intercession, sincere seeking and profound finding. It is the place where we are open to allowing God to touch our lives, and the lives of others through us. It is a state of being constantly open and attentive to God while being vigilant to avoid distractions.

+→ ←+

CHAPTER SEVENTEEN

The Temptation
of Busyness!

The Master said, "Martha, dear Martha,
you're fussing far too much
and getting yourself worked up over nothing.

LUKE 10:41, THE MESSAGE

IN OUR MODERN SOCIETY of promote-and-acquire, push-and-shove, a place of such quietness seems unnatural. Even for the few of us who do carve out some quiet time, it is often spent perusing busy schedules and attempting to make sense of all we are doing rather than truly focusing on God. Then, in the midst of all of this, we lapse somehow from even that little time alone with God because of the urgency of so many things we want to do. There are countless problems around us we believe only we can solve, whether at work, home, or even in the church we attend. The telephone rings, someone turns on the TV in the next room, the radio is blaring, the kids are screaming, and so forth. We are too exhausted most of the time to even focus. When we finally do get some quiet time to ourselves, the last thing we want to do is open our Bible to study, or seek the Lord in prayer for any length of time. We want to be distracted and entertained. We think it is only right for us to be able to relax during our down time. We don't think about what we are doing as we collapse on the couch in front of the television just to channel surf for an hour to two. Ultimately, we watch nothing but the changing images as we slowly drift off to sleep. After a while, when we are too tired to do anything else, we trudge off to bed.

Time before and after church gets lost in catching up on the latest gossip. Problems at home or work are the talk of the day. The drum of busyness beats faster and faster and we dance through a choreographed chaos that allows us anything but a quiet moment of reflection or thought. We react more than we act. Decisions are made by habit rather than conscious consideration. We choose to follow what other people say rather than finding the truth for ourselves, because it is so much easier. Our doctrine becomes whatever the preacher says and we even stop opening our Bible to follow along with the Scriptures as he is teaching. We just take for granted that he or she is quoting everything in context.

Then we work until we drop in order to fulfill the goals and purposes of others. We often find that their true aims were not the ideals which promote a dedicated Christian lifestyle. This disappointment and discouragement frequently lapses into bitterness, and then Self thrives as the ego becomes dominant and Jesus gets pushed further and further to the fringes. This and other fleshly fruit promote a religion of rules and regulations that ensnare the Believer and snuff out the reality of a vibrant relationship with Jesus. Legalism overshadows grace; fleshly indulgence seems more and more justifiable because it feels like such a needed relief from all our work. After all, look at how much *we* have accomplished!

Yet the truth is that we have replaced *accomplishment* with activity and mistaken busyness and urgency for truly living the Christ-life. We race faster and faster to do things of less and less significance to the kingdom of God. And because of this, all we have to look forward to will be one day digging up our single talent still caked with dirt and presenting it to Jesus. We smile as we say, "See, Lord, I still have it! Here it is!" He will only look at us sadly, shake His head. He will say "Oh you wicked and slothful servant . . ." (See Matthew 25:24-30.)

Satan couldn't be happier with all this sort of thing we do!

The Bible however tells us that we can be too busy and too wrapped up in things other than what God has for us:

> *Study to be quiet, and to do your own business, and to work with your own hands, as we commanded you; That ye may walk honestly toward them that are without, and that ye may have lack of nothing,* (I Thessalonians 4:11-12.)

Here, the Greek word *hesuchazo* translates as "quiet" which means "to rest, cease from labor. . . . to lead a quiet life, said of those who are not running hither and thither, but stay at home and mind their business."[22] Those who spend time with Jesus regularly have simplicity and focus to their lives which helps avoid pitfalls and becoming ensnared in the wrong kinds of activities. They find a place of rest in Christ.

As a rule, we are much busier than we need to be. We could be half as busy and accomplish twice as much if we would slow down and really spend time with Jesus! God has no heavy burdens for us.

> *Come unto me, all ye that labor and are heavy laden, and I will give you rest. Take my yoke upon you, and learn of me; for I am meek and lowly in heart: and ye shall find rest unto your souls. For my yoke is easy, and my burden is light,* (Matthew 11:28-30.)

We waste our time when we attempt to live our lives in the flesh with its limited strength!

Those plugged into Jesus are not overworked and stressed out all the time. The work of God is not too much to bear. God has help and rest for His people. We just never seem to enter into that rest because we put more faith in ourselves than we do in Jesus.

> *God's promise of entering his place of rest still stands, so we ought to tremble with fear that some of you might fail to get there. For this Good News—that God has prepared a place of rest—has been announced to us just as it was to them [the people of Israel in the desert with Moses]. But it did them no good because they didn't believe what God told them. . . .*
>
> *For all who enter into God's rest will find rest from their labors, just as God rested after creating the world. Let us do our best to enter that place of rest. For anyone who disobeys God, as the people of Israel did, will fall.*
>
> *For the word of God is full of living power. It is sharper than the sharpest knife, cutting deep into our innermost thoughts and desires. It exposes us for what*

we really are. Nothing in all creation can hide from him. Everything is naked and exposed before his eyes. This is the God to whom we must explain all that we have done.

That is why we have a great High Priest who has gone to heaven, Jesus the Son of God. Let us cling to him and never stop trusting him. This High Priest of ours understands our weaknesses, for he faced all of the same temptations we do, yet he did not sin. So let us come boldly to the throne of our gracious God. There we will receive his mercy, and we will find grace to help us when we need it, (Hebrews 4:1-2, 10-16 NLT.)

Those who enter into His rest cease from *their* labors and take up the Cross of Jesus Christ, whose burden is light. There is a time for work, but also a time for other things: family, church, and, yes, even leisure activities. As King Solomon in his wisdom wrote in Ecclesiastes 3:1, NLT: "For everything there is a season, a time for every activity under heaven."

It is never God's desire that you burn out. In fact, it has been my experience that God loves the minister more than the ministry and that if He has to shut down a church to save the faithful pastor from working him or herself to death, He will. I have even seen ministers resist Him in this, thinking they were being godly. If this is the way God feels about it, how much more should we prize and protect the gifts He has given us in the people who work in our ministries? (See Ephesians 4:8-12.) If we were truly being godly, then there would never be people abused and overworked in our churches!

This rest is also a result of the Word of God working in us to remove those things that are worthless or evil for the sake of things that bear eternal fruit, pleasing to God. This is the place of intense honesty before God where we will permit His Word to expose which things are fleshly and which are godly—it will show us a picture of what we really are! It will tear away the shroud of self-deception and help us see things clearly. It will expose ills in the light of truth allowing us to excise wasteful, decaying fruit and nurture life-giving fruit. Nothing will be hidden from us. We will no longer delude ourselves in thinking we are more than we really are, and our judgment will be sounder as we strive for the perfect will of God.

> *Therefore I urge you, brethren, by the mercies of God, to present your bodies a living and holy sacrifice, acceptable to God, which is your spiritual service of worship. And do not be conformed to this world, but be transformed by the renewing of your mind, so that you may prove what the will of God is, that which is good and acceptable and perfect. For through the grace given to me I say to everyone among you not to think more highly of himself than he ought to think; but to think so as to have sound judgment, as God has allotted to each a measure of faith,* (Romans 12:1-3 NASB.)

We are commanded not to conform to this world and the way it functions—to be *in the world but not of the world.* (See John 15:19.) This means that while we exist in a world that is frantic and over-stressed, we do not need to bear these pressures on our own. We can instead be focused on doing what God has called us to do and enjoying God's help in achieving it. It is interesting to note that the above passage comes just before a section describing how the parts of the Body of Christ are to work together:

For just as we have many members in one body and all the members do not have the same function, so we, who are many, are one body in Christ, and individually members one of another. Since we have gifts that differ according to the grace given to us, each of us is to exercise them accordingly, (Romans 12:4-6 NASB.)

God doesn't expect us to do it all alone, but He does expect us to do it all together, each carrying out our part and bearing the burdens of one another. With this, there will also be a time for rest. There will also be times of busyness as we go about our Father's work on earth, but with all this comes the grace to overcome. Never worry that you aren't doing enough, but do be concerned that you are not doing what you are supposed to do. This is where the peace and rest of God resides: in the continual presence of Jesus as we do His perfect will.

PRAY WITHOUT CEASING

Being with Jesus does start with regular times alone with Him and His Word. But if you leave Jesus in your prayer closet or quiet place, then you are still missing out on His ministry. Just as there is a time for seeking quiet with God, there is a time to accompany Him from that quiet place into the world—after all, how else will we help others if we don't take Him to them? Jesus admonished His disciples to:

Go therefore and make disciples of all the nations, baptizing them in the name of the Father and of the Son and of the Holy Spirit, (Matthew 28:19, NKJV.)

We should do no less.

Paul admonished us in the book of I Thessalonians 5:17 to "pray without ceasing." Does he mean to be continually on our knees in our prayer closet and never go out? Absolutely not! I believe it means taking the attitude and attentiveness of prayer with us wherever we go. Nothing should come out of our mouths that we wouldn't say to God in prayer. No situation we meet should pass by unresolved without it being placed before the throne of God. We should also be ever ready for God to speak to our hearts about what to do and how to solve such problems.

When you take time to be with Jesus, then He will go where you go and bring His power and wisdom to bear on any situation.

So I ask again, have you been with Jesus *today*?

Well, now is always the best time to start!

> *Behold, I stand at the door, and knock: if any man hear my voice, and open the door, I will come in to him, and will sup with him, and he with me. To him that over-cometh will I grant to sit with me in my throne, even as I also overcame, and am set down with my Father in his throne. He that hath an ear, let him hear what the Spirit saith unto the churches,* (Revelation 3:20-22.)

➤➤ ◄◄

CHAPTER EIGHTEEN

The *Greater* Commandment

. . . that the love wherewith thou hast loved me may be in them.

JOHN 17: 26

This is my commandment, That ye love
one another, as I have loved you.

JOHN 15:12

A WOMAN CAME TO JESUS with a costly box of perfume called spikenard; it was worth an entire year's wages. She broke the box and poured its contents over Christ's head so that every drop of oil fell upon Him. The religious men who witnessed her act grumbled that she'd wasted money, but Jesus was so moved, He said wherever His Gospel was preached, the story of her offering would be told. (See Matthew 26:6-13; Mark 14:1-9; and Luke 7:36-50.)

The box she broke wasn't itself the fragrant offering for Jesus. The woman didn't paint or polish the box to try to make it more acceptable to Him before she cracked it to release its costly contents. She didn't rub the box with perfume in order that it would smell like the spikenard inside. Instead, she broke the box so the purity of the nard inside the box could be released.

It is time we stopped paying so much attention to our outer flesh and started focusing on the most precious gift of Christ within us. It is only through releasing the power of Jesus within us that the world will experience His kingdom.

WE CANNOT LOVE LIKE JESUS
UNTIL WE BECOME BROKEN LIKE JESUS

The ninth and final prayer of Jesus in John 17 was "that the love wherewith thou hast loved me may be in them." (See John 17:23.) I do not believe that He prayed this prayer so that this love would stay bottled up inside us. He also commanded us to "love one another, as I have loved you," (John 15:12.) This love, when bottled up inside, is of little use to anyone no matter how much we embellish the outside of the bottle. Though we as Christians have this love within us from the time we are born again—"because the love of God is shed abroad in our hearts by the Holy Ghost which is given unto us" (see Romans 5:5)—most of us are so *self*-involved and *self*-absorbed that we never experience God's incredible love.

Where Self rules, there is no room for the love of God to work. Self on the throne is diametrically opposed to the love of God as described by Paul in I Corinthians 13. Look at each of the points the Apostle brings out in this passage:

> *Love is patient, love is kind and is not jealous;*
> *love does not brag and is not arrogant, does not act*
> *unbecomingly;*

it does not seek its own, is not provoked,
does not take into account a wrong suffered, does not
rejoice in unrighteousness,
but rejoices with the truth; bears all things, believes all
things, hopes all things,
endures all things. Love never fails,
(I Corinthians 13:4-8 NASB.)

Paul depicts the love of God as the most powerful force in the universe—something that never fails. No wonder Christians today are so powerless to change society—we have forgotten to utilize our unfailing Power Source.

In Ephesians 5, Paul uses the marriage as an analogy for the relationship between Christ and His church. (See Ephesians 5:18-33.) Somehow, in a time when over fifty percent of marriages in the U.S. end in divorce, this remains a vivid description of the state of the Church today. The major cause for divorce among married couples is the same reason many become divorced from Christ. As selfishness and extramarital affairs have killed many marriages, it is also destroying the mission of the Church in this age.

Love is the lubricant for the Body of Christ as described in Ephesians 4:16:

> *He makes the whole body fit together perfectly. As*
> *each part does its own special work, it helps the other*
> *parts grow, so that the whole body is healthy and grow-*
> *ing and full of love.*

Friction between parts of the Body chafes and grates without love. If this continues for long the pieces become warped, separated, and burned out, and its effectiveness grinds to a halt. Instead of operating like a well-oiled machine ushering in the kingdom of God, all it does is produce smoke which blinds our eyes to the very truth we were trying to teach. Just as love never fails, without love we always fail.

RELEASING THE LIFE OF GOD

For His life to be released through Jesus Christ, God the Son *chose* to come to the earth and die. We are to be followers of Christ's pattern. Our outer shell—the natural man—has to die in order for the inner man to be released. As long as we preserve that outer shell—keeping the flesh intact—the inner man will never be released. As long as we are imprisoned by that, we will never see the ministry of Jesus Christ come alive in and through us.

The Christian life is to be lived in the Spirit, not the flesh. We must crucify the flesh and die to Self so the Spirit of God can rule and reign in our lives. The Bible says it's like a seed that falls to the ground and dies, only to spring up again.

> *A grain of wheat must fall to the ground and die to make many seeds. But if it never dies, it remains only a single seed. Those who love their lives will lose them, but those who hate their lives in this world will keep true life forever,* (John 12:24-25 NASB.)

A seed is a container of life. As long as the seed coat remains intact, new life cannot spring forth. Some seeds lie dormant for decades with no growth and seemingly no purpose, until the outer shell is broken open so the seed can interact with soil and water. Once this happens it begins to grow. A seed can sit for a hundred years and accomplish nothing, but when a seed finally dies, the life from within that one seed can feed millions.

We spend much of our time and effort trying to be loved, and often miss the fact that we already have the most powerful love in the universe ready and waiting to burst forth. We keep looking to the clouds hoping for Jesus to come back in the flesh, instead He sits in our prayer closets waiting for us to enter in and spend time with Him. The eternal fate of all those around us rests on our ability to look past the mundane and temporary and live our Christian life as if we really believe in the eternal.

CHRISTIAN FICTION

It is amazing how much the popularity of Christian fiction has grown in the last few decades. From being a genre with little attention, it has become a popular item on the *New York Times* bestseller list. It would be easy to condemn this as being a distraction from reading the Bible or even Christian discipleship books designed to lead us closer to God. However, if we look more closely at the trend, I think we will see that it reveals a deeper hunger for God than we realized existed.

Why do I say this? How could it be that fiction stories show us anything about ourselves? Well, look at what these books are about. The *Left Behind* series launched one bestselling book after another, and fictional stories of spiritual warfare continue to sell year after year. Others write books along the same themes that have probably made the fiction section in the local Christian bookstore the fastest expanding section of all. Why is this?

I believe it is because Christians today are incredibly hungry to see the supernatural power of God at work in our everyday lives, and these books offer an opportunity to at least imagine having such a life. While the characters of these books walk through the end times or periods of spiritual significance from which we feel so far removed, we can vicariously imagine ourselves with God being active in our own lives.

The only problem is that we *are* living in the end times and now *is* the greatest period of spiritual significance the world has yet seen. There are more people on the earth today that need to make the decision between heaven and hell than in all previous history combined! It is time for us to stop living vicariously through fiction and start living God's will for real.

FULLY ARMED, EQUIPPED, AND READY TO BAIL OUT

So many Christians are like F-16 Eagle pilots who zoom around in the world's most powerfully equipped airplane. Every Sunday they show off incredible feats of operating in the heavenlies. Yet, at the first blip of trouble on the radar come Monday morning, they are groping for the ejection button. "Oh, brother," they say, "won't it be wonderful when Jesus finally comes back and raptures us out of this place and we can be with Him? Don't we truly have something to which we can look forward?"

Yes, we do have something wonderful to look forward to, but why look *forward* to it when we can be living it today? Why wait for Jesus to come back when He is already here? Why look for another time of miracles on the earth when He wants so badly to perform them today? The only ejection button we need is the one that will eject us out of the pilot's seat so that we can turn it back over to Jesus!

When we hear the word "egotistical" we often think of someone who pushes others around to get their way. While this is one part of being egotistical, it is but a small part. It actually means rejecting what God says about us because we believe more in our own opinions. We look into the Bible and say, "Well, yeah, that's true, but He must really mean that for someone else, not me." We say "I can't", "I shouldn't", "I'm not worthy to", "I would never dare", and more. We think we are being humble, but instead we are operating in the worst kind of pride: The kind that says we know more than God does!

If we spend time with Him in His Word, we can begin to see more clearly what God has for us. James calls the Word of God a mirror that will show us who we really are in Christ. If we refuse to do what we learn in those times of being with Jesus, then we are like someone who looks into a mirror and walks away, immediately forgetting what we look like. (See James 1:22-25.) This is looking fully into the face of God and saying, "No, God, that is not the way it is; it is really like this." We can't afford to let our weaknesses and ignorance hinder His strength.

I once flew to Cuba to preach a crusade when, in the darkness, I missed seeing a six foot high concrete arch. Being five inches taller than that gateway, I hit it full force, splitting my head open and causing me to bleed profusely. I had double vision during the entire sermon. (What a massive crowd!)

The next morning we flew to Amsterdam to witness in the red light district. My head was pounding with the worst headache imaginable. We landed, went out to Baines Bridge, and I asked the team to join me in prayer because I was in too much blinding pain and too exhausted to minister. As we gathered in a circle and held hands in prayer, prostitutes, drug addicts, and homosexuals moved closer to see who was in the center of the circle. More and more came until a large crowd had surrounded us. I don't know how many were saved that night, but it was a miracle. I discovered later I had suffered a severe concussion, but by then it didn't matter.

Now am I saying that even if you are badly injured you still need to minister for God no matter what? No, don't misunderstand why I am sharing this story. If you hurt yourself you still need to have wisdom and get help, which is exactly what I did once I realized I'd received a concussion. What I am saying is that we often neglect to serve God because we feel we are too weak or too uneducated, not realizing that admitting our lack is more help than hindrance. Our weakness succumbs to His strength. God desires to do great things through us, if we are only willing to be with Him, walking where He tells us to walk, and letting His love flow through us.

WHAT CAN SEPARATE US FROM THE LOVE OF GOD?

Ego on the throne has hindered the operation of God's love in our lives. Whether we insist on our own way or hide humbly behind our inabilities while rejecting His abilities, we are allowing ego to firmly remain on the throne of our lives. We deceive ourselves into thinking we are doing right. Susannah Wesley, the mother of revivalists John and Charles Wesley, once said, "Religion is nothing else than doing the will of God and not our own. Heaven or hell depends on this alone." It is just that simple. Yet instead of doing God's will daily, we smother truth and love by wrapping it tightly in religious jargon, trying to justify our inactivity and disobedience. We may say, "Oh, brother, it is so hard to live a Christian life!" It is not hard to live a Christian life—it is impossible. That is why we have to let Jesus live it through us.

Ego dressed in this cloak of religion is poisonous. It is the proverbial wolf in sheep's clothing. We must daily empty ourselves of this ego—the big "I". We must look long and hard in the mirror of God's Word, remembering what we saw after we walk away. The surety of the Father's love within us is too often hindered by ego. Only by shattering this false exterior can we release His love to those around us. That love is what keeps the present-day ministry of Christ flowing through us and oils the points where we come into contact with others in His Body. This allows us to effectively work together to manifest His kingdom on earth.

Too often, however, the opposite is true: Shrouded in our cloak of religious egotism, we practice sanctified revenge. In the name of Jesus, we stab those in the back who oppose us, because we feel threatened or intimidated. We then justify turning away from them. It is at that point the joints and parts begin to simmer from the friction and warp or break apart.

Things from without cannot keep us from the love of God, only things from within. Look at what Paul said about this at the end of Romans 8:

> We know that God causes everything to work together for the good of those who love God and are called according to his purpose for them. For God knew his people in advance, and he chose them to become like his Son, so that his Son would be the firstborn, with many brothers and sisters. And having chosen them, he called them to come to him. And he gave them right standing with himself, and he promised them his glory.
>
> What can we say about such wonderful things as these? If God is for us, who can ever be against us? Since God did not spare even his own Son but gave him up for us all, won't God, who gave us Christ, also give us everything else? . . .
>
> Can anything ever separate us from Christ's love?

Does it mean he no longer loves us if we have trouble or calamity, or are persecuted, or are hungry or cold or in danger or threatened with death? (Even the Scriptures say, "For your sake we are killed every day; we are being slaughtered like sheep.") No, despite all these things, overwhelming victory is ours through Christ, who loved us.

And I am convinced that nothing can ever separate us from his love. Death can't, and life can't. The angels can't, and the demons can't. Our fears for today, our worries about tomorrow, and even the powers of hell can't keep God's love away. Whether we are high above the sky or in the deepest ocean, nothing in all creation will ever be able to separate us from the love of God that is revealed in Christ Jesus our Lord, (Romans 8:28-32, 35-39 NLT.)

No, nothing can separate us from His love, but we can refuse to release it in our lives by letting it be smothered by our own fleshly pursuits. We restrict the work of God and reject the prayer of Jesus in John 17 by ignoring the *greater* commandment:

> *I command you to love each other in the same way that I love you,* (John 15:12.)

Until we release this kind of love, we will never do the same works—much less the greater works—that Jesus did. It is time we activated this last prayer of Jesus and release the love He has so bountifully poured out on us into the world around us. This love is the foundation of His kingdom. It is time that we began to fully live its reality, and then watch what happens. Jesus' works are much closer than you have ever imagined!

➤➤ ◄◄

CHAPTER NINETEEN

Will You Be Part of Answering the Prayers of Jesus?

*Verily, verily, I say unto you, He that believeth on me,
the works that I do shall he do also; and greater works
than these shall he do; because I go to my Father.*

JOHN 14:12

*If two of you shall agree on earth as touching any thing
that they shall ask, it shall be done for them of my Father
which is in heaven. For where two or three are gathered
together in my name, there am I in the midst of them.*

MATTHEW 18:19-20

THERE IS A UNIQUE CALLING from God on your life—a
plan He has for no one else. What you do with it is up to you. Will you
bury it in the ground as did the servant with one talent? (Matthew
25:14-30.) Will you come into agreement with the prayers of Jesus
and be part of the answer? Or will you continue to live with Self
on the throne—with its hurts, ego, deficiencies, selfishness, deception, and its clouded, narrow-minded worldview ruling your life?
Though the issues of knowing and living God's plan for your life

may seem complex, the actual decision is really very basic: Will you live this day—this hour, this minute, this breath—with Jesus as Lord of your life, or do you think you can do better on your own?

This is the moment to make the decision that will influence this and every moment following for the remainder of your life. It may be difficult, but I wouldn't want to live any other way!

Recently, I heard about a football player who had the personal motto: "No one will work harder than I do today." It was a motto that took him to Harvard on an academic scholarship after having been born into a family that could never have otherwise afforded it. This motto brought him to a starting position on an NFL team even though Harvard is rarely a place an NFL scout finds great talent.

We should have a similar motto that is just as simple: "Today I will seek God in order to do His will."

One of Satan's greatest ploys is to make us believe that living the Christ-life is out of our reach. He would have us idolize certain men and women of God just as a teenager might idolize a rock star or sports hero. He would have us think, "Oh, if I could only be like them! But it must take such great talent and determination to do what they do. It is so far beyond anything I could ever do!"

Well, there is the deception: *If I could only be like them.* Well, guess what? You *are* like them! If you are a Christian, then you have inside you the same Holy Spirit others have. You too have Jesus as Lord and Savior, and you have a heavenly Father who loves you and wants to know and be known by you. In God's eyes, all that matters is your obedience to His will. Large meetings don't matter. Big churches don't matter. Incredible mission outreaches don't matter. If they are of God, then they are merely byproducts of Believers who have obeyed Him. *The important thing is the obedience.*

Except the LORD build the house, they labor in vain that build it: except the LORD keep the city, the watchman waketh but in vain. It is vain for you to rise up early, to sit up late, to eat the bread of sorrows: for so he giveth his beloved sleep, (Psalm 127:1-2.)

We can work hard, stay up late, rise early, work at the church 120 out of the 168 hours in a week, but none of it matters if we are building a kingdom unto ourselves rather than unto God. In fact, the opposite is true: If we are obeying God, then we won't be working impossibly long hours to build His kingdom, because He gives His beloved sleep and rest. The only real work is staying in our quiet place until we learn His will. Then we simply have to live it out. The rest will take care of itself.

We need to come into agreement with God and His Word. We need to come into agreement with the prayers of Jesus.

THE POWER OF AGREEMENT

The works of Jesus—and greater works—will only come to the Church when we as Christians come into agreement with His Word, His will, and the nine prayers from John 17. We need to seek His face sincerely to know what He wants us to do. God is waiting for those who dare to draw close to Him. Are you willing be faithful to God and press in close to Him until Jesus' nine prayers are really and truly answered?

1) "THAT THEY MAY KNOW THE ONLY TRUE GOD," (JOHN 17:3.)

We cannot be content with knowing *about* God or what *others* think of Him. This is dead religion and self-worship. We have to take the risk of spending time with Jesus and His Word and learn to really know Him, His heart, His ministry, and then *just do it*. We will never know God, until we seek Him with all of our hearts.

> *"You will seek Me and find Me when you search for Me*
> *with all your heart. I will be found by you," declares the*
> LORD, (Jeremiah 29:13-14 NASB.)

2) "THAT THEY MAY BE ONE," (JOHN 17:21.)

Division comes from not being one with Jesus. If we were one with Him then we would take our proper place within His Body. If we are ever to have unity in the Church, it will not be through ecumenical movements that water down the truth in order for it to be more accepted by others. Only when we are one with Jesus will we be one with each other. Each of us must first learn our individual place in His plan. Only then can each part be "fitly joined together" (see Ephesians 4:16) to realize His kingdom on the earth.

> *Under his direction, the whole body is fitted together*
> *perfectly. As each part does its own special work, it helps*
> *the other parts grow, so that the whole body is healthy*
> *and growing and full of love,* (Ephesians 4:16 NLT.)

3) "THAT THEY MIGHT HAVE MY JOY," (JOHN 17:13.)

We don't have His joy because we are trying to live by our flesh and its deceptive desires. His joy is not a fruit of the flesh, but of His Spirit (see Galatians 5:22) and comes from doing His will. When we live by

His Spirit and give Him our emotions and desires, there is nothing the devil can do to us to steal our peace and joy. We have "joy unspeakable and full of glory," (see I Peter 8:8) because we celebrate the Christ within as become part of manifesting His kingdom on earth.

> *When you obey me, you remain in my love, just as I obey my Father and remain in his love. I have told you this so that you will be filled with my joy. Yes, your joy will overflow!* (John 15:10-11 NLT.)

4) "THAT YOU SHOULDEST KEEP THEM FROM EVIL," (JOHN 17:15.)

Proverbs says, "The complacency of fools will destroy them," (Proverbs 1:22 NASB.) When we become comfortable in our flesh or accept its dictate that we cannot live like Jesus, then we give evil free reign in both our own lives and our communities. We adopt the tone, "Well, there is really nothing that I can do about it! I wonder what's on TV tonight." We accept being entertained rather than fulfilled. This complacency breeds spiritual poverty.

If we are ever to be a threat to evil rather than having evil be a threat to us, then we must learn that our new nature in Christ has obliterated our past, and given us *new* values and a *new* life. Because of this, we now supernaturally have a *new* present and future! Child-like obedience to His direction can usher in His present-day ministry, vanquish evil and establish His will and kingdom around us.

> *My brothers, be all the more eager to make your call-ing and election sure. For if you do these things, you will never fall, and you will receive a rich welcome into the*

eternal kingdom of our Lord and Savior Jesus Christ, (II Peter 1:10-11 NIV.)

5) "THAT THEY MIGHT BE SANCTIFIED THROUGH THE TRUTH," (JOHN 17:19.)

Do we live by truth? Are we brutally honest with ourselves at all times? Are we willing to go through Christ's daily pruning to cut off that which is dead so that we may bear more fruit? (See John 15: 1-8.) Loving the truth is the key to living out the present-day ministry of Jesus. Those who believe or accept half-truths lapse into complacency and self-contentment. They are satisfied with where they are and care little about pressing in to seek God's will and His desires. People who love truth are not afraid of letting others see their weaknesses or humanity. In fact, they are able to glorify God as His strength can be seen through their weakness! It is not a special anointing that counts, but having been with the Anointed One—Jesus Christ.[23]

> *Since God has so generously let us in on what he is doing, we're not about to throw up our hands and walk off the job just because we run into occasional hard times. We refuse to wear masks and play games. We don't maneuver and manipulate behind the scenes. And we don't twist God's Word to suit ourselves. Rather, we keep everything we do and say out in the open, the whole truth on display, so that those who want to can see and judge for themselves in the presence of God,* (II Corinthians 4:1-2 THE MESSAGE.)

6) "THAT THEY MAY BEHOLD MY GLORY," (JOHN 17:24.)

God's glory has appeared from time to time on the earth as men, women, and children have humbled themselves before God, sincerely seeking His presence, and repenting of their fleshly lives. But repentance alone has never kept God's glory and revival growing. It has always been limited to a certain place for a certain time. It has always been quenched as we have turned back to our flesh for answers, thinking we can provide the necessary discipline to reach heaven.

The Bible is clear on this: It is not what we don't do, it is what we do. It is time for a generation that will forsake the flesh and rise to walk in the Spirit, empowered by His gifts and gifted by His power. Only then will the fruit of His glory take root and flourish throughout the earth.

> *All of us have had that veil removed so that we can be mirrors that brightly reflect the glory of the Lord. And as the Spirit of the Lord works within us, we become more and more like him and reflect his glory even more,* (II Corinthians 3:18 NLT.)

7) "THAT THEY MAY BE MADE PERFECT," (JOHN 17:23.)

The only perfect person is a dead person. We have been crucified, buried, and resurrected with Christ. It is no longer we who live, but Christ who lives in and through us. (See Galatians 2:20.) We must let the Christ-life flow through us so that we can be revived as was the valley of dry bones before Ezekiel. (See Ezekiel 37:1-14.) Are we willing to leave the rotting corpse of our flesh behind and move forward with

His Spirit into God's holiness and perfection, being made into a vessel "meet for the master's use"? (See II Timothy 2:21.)

> *Be sober, be vigilant; because your adversary the devil, as a roaring lion, walketh about, seeking whom he may devour: Whom resist steadfast in the faith, knowing that the same afflictions are accomplished in your brethren that are in the world.*
>
> *But the God of all grace, who hath called us unto his eternal glory by Christ Jesus, after that ye have suffered a while, make you perfect, establish, strengthen, settle you,* (I Peter 5:8-10.)

8) THAT THE WORLD WOULD KNOW THAT WE HAVE "BEEN WITH JESUS."
(SEE ACTS 4:13 AND JOHN 17:22-23, 25.)

The world could see that the apostles had been with Jesus. Even Peter's shadow had been empowered with healing after he had been with Jesus. (See Acts 5:15.) And, lest we think that walking the earth with Jesus was the only way to qualify for walking in His anointing, remember Paul spread even more of Christ around the world than did the Twelve who had spent time with Jesus before and after His crucifixion. Paul had only met the Messiah *after* He ascended.

It is time to press into Him until the world sees the love of Jesus shining on our face, and as a result, is born again.

> *When they saw the courage of Peter and John and realized that they were unschooled, ordinary men, they*

were astonished and they took note that these men had
been with Jesus, (Acts 4:13 NIV.)

9) "THAT THE LOVE WITH WHICH YOU LOVED ME MAY BE IN THEM," (JOHN 17:26.)

As we reveal Christ to a desperate world, we reveal that supernatural love which embraces and heals. We can no longer be content to focus on the outside, polishing, painting, and admiring the container of spikenard as if it were of more value than the perfume of His love from within. It is time to shatter the worship of outside appearances and allow the love of God (see Romans 5:5) within us to flow forth, as well as His righteousness, and His kingdom. We cannot ignore the greater commandment of Jesus: We must love others with the same love with which He loves us.

> *Beloved, let us love one another: for love is of God; and*
> *every one that loveth is born of God, and knoweth God.*
> *He that loveth not knoweth not God; for God is love. In*
> *this was manifested the love of God toward us, because*
> *that God sent his only begotten Son into the world, that*
> *we might live through him,* (I John 4:7-9.)

JESUS HAS DELEGATED IT TO *US*!

As we join Christ in prayer, we gain the power to say, "Look on us" because we've been with Jesus. Alone with our Lord, we take on His characteristics. His presence and power causes demons to tremble and mountains to quake. The last great blow to the devil will be when the saints no longer appear as Joe, Shirley, Marco, or Latisha, but we all look just like Jesus—transformed because we've spent time with Him!

Who will do greater works than Jesus? People who are His representatives—who have seen Him, been with Him, and spent time with Him through prayer, meditating on His Word, praising him, repenting from dead works, and being totally vulnerable before Him.

Jesus returned to the Father and now sits at His right hand. He is sitting because He has delegated His mission to you and me, and has faith that we will carry it out.

Imagine God asking you to give everything you owned—including your name—to someone else who would do more with it than you. Imagine giving your talent, your career, your family, your possessions, your reputation, everything you've ever been, plus everything you could potentially become, to another person. Jesus Christ delegated everything He had—His power, His reputation, His Name, His life, His history, His Words, His very Spirit, everything He'd ever been and everything He ever would be—and gave it all to us.

Jesus Christ gave His ministry to the weakest Believer in the Body of Christ—the rights to His Name, the keys to His Kingdom, all His authority over the earth, and all power to represent Him on this earth. That person can abuse the power, misrepresent Christ's Name, exploit His reputation, or choose not to do one thing with what Jesus gave—it is that person's choice. It is our choice as well.

Christ departed physically from the earth to sit—yes, sit—at the Father's right hand in heaven. Why? Jesus *knew*—beyond any shadow of doubt—there would come a day when the people who are called by His Name will stand up and fulfill *all* His prophecies and answer *all* His prayers:

Signs, wonders, and miracles will follow them that believe. (See Mark 16:17-18.)

The works I've done shall you do and greater works than I shall ye do because I go unto My Father, (John 14:12.)

If you ask anything in My name, My Father will do it, (John 14:14.)

If two agree as touching anything, it will be done, (Matthew 18:19.)

Till we all come unto the measure of the stature of the fullness of Christ, (Ephesians 4:13.)

That they may be one, even as we are one: I in them, and thou in me, that they may be made perfect in one and that the world may know that thou hast sent Me, (John 17:21.)

That Christ may present the Church to Himself, as a glorious Church, not having spot or wrinkle or any such thing; but that the Church should be holy without blemish, (Ephesians 5:27.)

We have yet to see all His prayers answered and all His prophecies fulfilled, but we will. Christ's power resides within *us* as Believers! We say when we accept Christ as Savior, "Come into my heart Lord Jesus." It's time to start believing He really did. When Self is completely off the throne and the barrier around our heart comes down, then the present-day ministry of Jesus Christ is released. That's why

Paul said, "I die daily." (See I Corinthians 15:31.) He knew the Self-life was the greatest enemy of the Christ-life.

OUR GENERATION WILL USHER
IN CHRIST'S RETURN

Jesus knew His death and resurrection was the greatest blow to Satan. The second greatest blow will come when Believers, filled with Christ's Spirit, unite and multiply, thus allowing the present-day ministry of Jesus to flow through us and go beyond what we might ever see or imagine.

Many years ago at the Waldorf Astoria in New York City, Prime Minister Begin, who won the Nobel Peace Prize, invited me to host the only Christian delegation with whom he would meet during that trip to the States. I invited thirty-two men and women who I knew to be intercessors to join me. This group included Ann Murchison whose husband owned the Dallas Cowboys, and a wonderful couple, Kyffin and Roberta Simpson, precious Believers from Barbados and others. While in the company of Prime Minister Begin, I asked Ann Murchison to read some scriptures.

As she read, the presence of Jesus entered that room. Prime Minister Begin began to weep. Introductions were still being made, and those who stood could scarcely talk for weeping as well. The anointing grew so strong that the Prime Minister finally stood up, and with tears streaming down his face said, "The Spirit I sense in this room is the Spirit of the redemption of Israel." All of those in the room had humbled themselves before God. Christ was highly exalted and His glory filled the room.

All began to weep—including Dr. Ben Armstrong, the Executive Director of the National Religious Broadcasters, and Forrest Montgomery, the attorney for the National Association of

Evangelicals. We could see the manifestation of the prophecy of King Solomon in II Chronicles 7:14: "If my people, who are called by my name, will humble themselves and pray and seek my face and turn from their wicked ways, then will I hear from heaven and will forgive their sin and will heal their land." It seemed as if the prophecy was being fulfilled before our very eyes. The spirit the Prime Minister described was not only the spirit of the redemption of Israel, but of America, also.

Yes, you and I can be with Jesus and be changed! But it will not happen until we admit that we are not where we need to be with Him. Only then can we allow Jesus to work through us in order that His divine will and purpose can be manifested.

We can preach repentance while dressed like John the Baptist (see Mark 1:6) and still become a stench in the nostrils of God— intoxicated with our own opinions. The living Christ in us has a divine schedule, passion, and purpose to manifest on this earth. It will come through the same explosion of glory with which He manifested Himself two thousand years ago.

The sole reason Jesus left this earth was to send His Spirit to us. "It is expedient for you that I go away: for if I go not away, the Comforter will not come unto you; but if I depart, I will send him unto you," (John 16:7.) The ultimate mission of the Person of the Holy Spirit is not to give *us* a gift; the great mission of the Holy Spirit is to manifest Jesus and all His glory *in* and *through* us!

When the Father sees Jesus abiding within us through His Spirit, all of heaven is authorized and mobilized to empower us to fulfill Christ's mission. Satan fears millions of Believers operating in the full measure of the Spirit of God, which will shatter his earthly reign.

When we've been with Jesus, we will be transformed into His

likeness. (See Ephesians 4:13.) Satan cannot distinguish our face from that of Jesus. Incredible authority and power comes upon us—the type of power Christ said would enable His followers to do greater works than He.

Jesus testified He did only what He saw the Father do, and spoke only what He heard the Father speak. When we hear what Jesus hears, see what He sees, we will do what He did and speak with the same authority with which He spoke.

Jesus prayed, *"I brought You glory on earth by completing the work You gave Me to do,"* (John 17:4 NIV.) Christ's purpose was, and still is, to bring glory to the Father. Because Christ gave His ministry to us, our destiny is also to glorify God, which releases the power of heaven.

> *And I will do whatever you ask in My name, so that*
> *the Son may bring glory to the Father, you may ask any-*
> *thing in My Name and I will do it,* (John 14:13-14 NIV.)

Our generation will see the manifestation of the power Christ gave us. He fully intends to fulfill His present-day ministry. It's all about Jesus.

Jesus said, "Take up your cross and follow Me." (See Matthew 16:24; Mark 8:34; and Luke 19:22.)

Will you accept His call?

ENDNOTES

→→ ←←

1. Vine, W. E., Merrill F. Unger, and William White. *Vine's Complete Expository Dictionary of Old and New Testament Words*, Vol. 1. (Thomas Nelson, Nashville, 1996), s.v. "To Know," 131.

2. David B. Barrett et al., ed., *World Christian Encyclopedia: A Comparative Survey of Churches and Religions in the Modern World*, Second Edition.Vol. 1. (New York: Oxford University Press, 2001), 10.

3. If not, you can find the text on line at http://www.greatcom.org/laws/ or http://www.crusade.org/fourlaws/.

4. For example, the woman at the well in John 4, the Syrophenician woman in Mark 7:25-30, and the Roman centurion in Luke 7:1-10.

5. Vine et. al., Vol. 1., s.v. "Amen," 25.

6. Vine et al., Vol. 1, s.v. "Together," 263.

7. For more information on Psalm 133, see *The Commanded Blessing* by Dr. Michael Evans.

8. Vine et al., Vol. 2, s.v. "Joy (Noun and Verb), Joyfulness, Joyfully, Joyous," 336.

9. Barret et. al, *World Christian Encyclopedia*, Vol. 1, 11.

10. Achtemeier, Paul J., Harper's Bible Dictionary, 1st ed. (San Francisco: Harper & Row, and Society of Biblical Literature. 1985.), 287.

11. Vine, W. E., et al., Vol. 2, sv. "Money (love of)," 415.

12. Douglas, J.D. *New Bible Dictionary*. (Wheaton, IL: Tyndale House, 1996, 1982), 357.

13. Merriam-Webster, Inc. *Merriam-Webster's Collegiate Dictionary*. 10th ed. (Springfield, MA: Merriam-Webster, 1996, c1993), s.v., "Hypocrisy."

14. Vine et al., Vol. 2, s.v. "Hallow", 287.

15. Referring to Acts 2:16 where Peter told those gathered that "This is that which was prophesied" (paraphrase). Rev. Wilkerson's reference to this verse means that this is not yet the fullness of what God will be doing in these last days, but merely the beginning, as it was on the day of Pentecost when Peter spoke this verse.

16. Strong, James. Enhanced Strong's Lexicon, (Ontario: Woodside Bible Fellowship, 1996), s.v., "H8549 tamiym."

17. Ibid., s.v., "G5048 Teleioo."

18. Ibid., s.v., "G5046 Teleios."

19. Vine, et. al., Vol. 2, s.v., "Perfection, Perfecting (noun), Perfectness," 467.

20. Francis A. Schaeffer, The Mark of a Christian (Downers Grove, IL: InterVarsity Press), pp. 25, 35.

21. Strong, *Enhanced Strong's Lexicon*, s.v., "H7503 raphah."

22. Strong, *Enhanced Strong's Lexicon*, "G2270 hesuchazo."

23. According to Vine's, "Christ" means "anointed." (Vine's, Vol. 2, s.v. "Christ," 101.)

BIBLIOGRAPHY

Achtemeier, Paul J., *Harper's Bible Dictionary*, First Edition. San Francisco: Harper & Row, and Society of Biblical Literature. 1985.

Barrett, David B.; Kurian, George T.; and Johnson, Todd M.; eds. *World Christian Encyclopedia: A Comparative Survey of Churches and Religions in the Modern World*, Second Edition. New York: Oxford University Press, 2001.

Douglas, J.D. *New Bible Dictionary*. Wheaton, IL: Tyndale House, 1996, 1982.

Merriam-Webster, Inc. *Merriam-Webster's Collegiate Dictionary*. 10th ed. Springfield, MA: Merriam-Webster, 1996, c1993.

Strong, James. *Enhanced Strong's Lexicon*. Ontario: Woodside Bible Fellowship, 1996.

Vine, W. E., Merrill F. Unger, and William White. *Vine's Complete Expository Dictionary of Old and New Testament Words*, Volumes One and Two. Nashville: T. Nelson, 1996.

MICHAEL DAVID EVANS, the #1 *New York Times* bestselling author, is an award-winning journalist/Middle East analyst. Dr. Evans has appeared on hundreds of network television and radio shows including *Good Morning America, Crossfire* and *Nightline,* and *The Rush Limbaugh Show,* and on Fox Network, *CNN World News,* NBC, ABC, and CBS. His articles have been published in the *Wall Street Journal, USA Today, Washington Times, Jerusalem Post* and newspapers worldwide. More than twenty-five million copies of his books are in print, and he is the award-winning producer of nine documentaries based on his books.

Dr. Evans is considered one of the world's leading experts on Israel and the Middle East, and is one of the most sought-after speakers on that subject. He is the chairman of the board of the Ten Boom Holocaust Museum in Haarlem, Holland, and is the founder of Israel's first Christian museum—Friends of Zion: Heroes and History—in Jerusalem.

Dr. Evans has authored a number of books including: *History of Christian Zionism, Showdown with Nuclear Iran, Atomic Iran, The Next Move Beyond Iraq, The Final Move Beyond Iraq,* and *Countdown.* His body of work also includes the novels *Seven Days, GameChanger, The Samson Option, The Four Horsemen, The Locket,* and his most recent, *Born Again: 1967.*

↣   ↢

Michael David Evans is available to speak or for interviews.
Contact: EVENTS@drmichaeldevans.com.

BOOKS BY: MIKE EVANS

Israel: America's Key to Survival

Save Jerusalem

The Return

Jerusalem D.C.

Purity and Peace of Mind

Who Cries for the Hurting?

Living Fear Free

I Shall Not Want

Let My People Go

Jerusalem Betrayed

Seven Years of Shaking: A Vision

The Nuclear Bomb of Islam

Jerusalem Prophecies

Pray For Peace of Jerusalem

*America's War: The Beginning
of the End*

The Jerusalem Scroll

The Prayer of David

The Unanswered Prayers of Jesus

God Wrestling

The American Prophecies

Beyond Iraq: The Next Move

The Final Move beyond Iraq

Showdown with Nuclear Iran

*Jimmy Carter: The Liberal Left
and World Chaos*

Atomic Iran

Cursed

Betrayed

The Light

Corrie's Reflections & Meditations

GAMECHANGER SERIES:
GameChanger
Samson Option
The Four Horsemen

THE PROTOCOLS SERIES:
The Protocols
The Candidate

The Revolution

The Final Generation

Seven Days

The Locket

Living in the F.O.G.

Persia: The Final Jihad

Jerusalem

The History of Christian Zionism

Countdown

Ten Boom: Betsie, Promise of God

Commanded Blessing

Born Again: 1948
Born Again: 1967

Presidents in Prophecy

Stand with Israel

Prayer, Power and Purpose

COMING SOON:
Turning Your Pain Into Gain

The Columbus Code

Christopher Columbus, Secret Jew

TO PURCHASE, CONTACT: orders@timeworthybooks.com
P. O. BOX 30000, PHOENIX, AZ 85046